HANDBOOK TO
THE HEART OF CULTURE

VOLUME I

HANDBOOK TO THE HEART OF CULTURE

*A Guide for Cultivating the Soil
of Catholic Culture and Education*

REFLECTIONS AND PRACTICAL APPLICATIONS

VOLUME I:
PAIDEIA TO MONASTIC EDUCATION

GWEN ADAMS, PHD

HABIGER INSTITUTE FOR CATHOLIC LEADERSHIP

∽ ∼

CLUNY
Providence, Rhode Island

CLUNY EDITION, 2025

For information regarding The Habiger Institute for Catholic Leadership, please visit WWW.STTHOMAS.EDU/HABIGER.

For bulk orders of the *Handbook to The Heart of Culture* volumes, *The Heart of Culture*, or other Habiger Institute titles, please email SALES@CLUNYMEDIA.COM.

For more information regarding this title or any other Cluny publication, please write to info@clunymedia.com, or to Cluny Media LLC, P.O. Box 1664, Providence, RI 02901

Online at WWW.CLUNYMEDIA.COM

Handbook to The Heart of Culture, Volumes I, II, & III
copyright © 2024 Gwen Adams

The Heart of Culture copyright © 2020 Sophia Consulting LLC

Cluny editions of the same copyright © 2020 & 2025 Cluny Media LLC

ALL RIGHTS RESERVED

Scripture quotations are from the *New Revised Standard Version Bible: Catholic Edition*, copyright © 1989, 1993 National Council of the Churches of Christ in the United States of America. Used by permission. All rights reserved worldwide.

ISBN: 978-1685954031

Cover design by Clarke & Clarke
Cover image: Raphael, detail from *The School of Athens*, fresco, between 1509 and 1511

for my teachers

JDZ, COB, JR, *and* MJK

ACKNOWLEDGMENTS

I WOULD LIKE TO THANK the educational leaders who made time to discuss Catholic educational renewal for this work: Michael Naughton, Emily Dahdah, Raymond Hain, Fr. Thomas Haan, Dale Ahlquist, Christopher Fisher, Elisabeth Sullivan, Christopher Blum, and Andrew Seeley. I owe a special debt to Michael Naughton, Emily Dahdah, and Fr. Michael Keating for reading the early draft and offering advice and assistance all along the way.

Thanks go to John Emmet Clarke and everyone at Cluny Media. Thanks go also to Fr. Thomas Haan, Fr. Clayton Thompson, Fr. Elliot Żak, and Fr. Matthew Jakupco for taking time to explore the material that went into these volumes. Their pastoral and school experience, insights, and questions improved this work significantly.

I would like to thank all my teachers and mentors, from the good people at Maryvale Institute, especially Catherine Knowles and Mary Mills, and the faculty of Catholic Studies at the University of St. Thomas, the Angelicum, Christendom College, and Trinity School, especially Fr. Paul Murray, Jon Balsbaugh, Penny Arndt, David O'Hanley, Timothy

1

HANDBOOK TO THE HEART OF CULTURE

Nauman, Tom Finke, and Bridget Donohue, all the way back to my parents who homeschooled me, taught me to read and write, and named me for a character in a great play.

Finally, I am grateful to all the students I have had the privilege to teach, from everyone who ever took my course "Catholic Education: Ends, Principles, and Methods" to my wonderful middle school students. It is a pleasure to learn with and from you.

> Glory, science, knowledge, and whatever other fine names we use, never healed a wounded heart, nor changed a sinful one; but the Divine Word is with power.... Each one of us has lit his lamp from his neighbour, or received it from his fathers, and the lights thus transmitted are at this time as strong and as clear as if 1800 years had not passed since the kindling of the sacred flame.
>
> John Henry Newman,
> "The Tamworth Reading Room"

Gwen Adams
8 AUGUST 2024
FEAST OF ST. DOMINIC

INTRODUCTION TO THE SERIES

Handbook to *The Heart of Culture*

〜 〜

I HAVE READ *The Heart of Culture* many times, always with gratitude to the great teachers who people its chapters and the great teachers I have had. Christendom College (Front Royal, Virginia) introduced me to Jonathan Reyes and Christopher Blum. Jonathan Reyes taught my first course on Catholic education. Christopher Blum taught me about Catholic culture and was the one to recommend the Catholic Studies Program at the University of St. Thomas (St. Paul, Minnesota). There I wrote my thesis under Fr. Michael Keating and attended the first iteration of his course, the one that laid the foundations for *The Heart of Culture*.

In the afterword to *The Heart of Culture*, Jonathan Reyes points to the deep sense of hope that the book has inspired since its 2020 publication. These volumes aim to fortify that hope with stories of renewal, spiritual reflections, and practical applications. Each volume reviews part of the story told in *The Heart of Culture* with particular attention to the education of children and adolescents. Each volume offers a reflection on a virtue important for Catholic education. Each volume closes with chapters on pedagogy, content, and resources. The volumes aim to strike a balance so that new and experienced educators will find something of use: insights and inspiration in the reflection chapters, tools and skills in the Workbook chapters.

If you explore the resources, follow the advice of Basil and John Henry Newman. Sift the resources with discernment. Some resources are drawn directly from the Catholic educational tradition. Others have elements which can be baptized. Take what is helpful to serve the mission of Catholic education.

These volumes are in no way exhaustive. I already foresee a second edition in which others collaborate to add chapters on mathematics, music, languages, etc. I have concentrated on the tools I know best. These are not necessarily the best tools, nor the only ones. Nor should the reader feel bound to use all the tools, all the time. I use one tool, then another, as time permits. In some years, I have concentrated more on cultivating integration than on seminar method. In other years, I was so busy writing lectures I had no time to improve them. Feel free to pick and choose, experiment, and adjust the ideas to your own needs and schedule. In some ways, teaching is like cooking. I have written out directions the way I would write out directions for making a roux, granting the reader full permission to adapt, skip, reorder, or otherwise improve upon the directions. Sometimes you must make a roux several times before you understand the recipe. By that time, you know better than the recipe. Make these "recipes" your own.

The volumes follow a three-part structure as follows:

Volume I: *Paideia to Monastic Education*

Volume I: *Paideia* to Monastic Education (pairing with
The Heart of Culture, Introduction–Chapter Four)
  Introduction to the Series
  Part 1: Reflections
  Chapter I: Israel and Greek *Paideia*
  Chapter II: Christ, the Early Church, and Monasticism
  Chapter III: A Reflection on Sensory-Emotional
    Formation, Wonder, and Studiousness
  Part 2: The Workbook
  Chapter I: Cultivating Wonder: A Practical Guide to
    Sensory-Emotional Formation
  Chapter II: Physical Education, Song, Dance, and
    Manual Labor
  Chapter III: Nature Study and Journaling
  Chapter IV: Reading Aloud
  Chapter V: Leading a Socratic Discussion: A Variation
    on Didactic Instruction
  Chapter VI: Assignments, Projects, and Activities from
    Paideia to Monastic Education
  Chapter VII: Further Reading and Resources
  Conclusion to Volume I

Volume II: The Medieval World to the Renaissance-Baroque
  Era (pairing with *The Heart of Culture*, Chapters Five–Six)
  Introduction to Volume II
  Part 1: Reflections
  Chapter I: The Medieval World
  Chapter II: The Renaissance and Baroque Era
  Chapter III: A Reflection on Docility
  Part 2: The Workbook

HANDBOOK TO THE HEART OF CULTURE

Chapter I: Cultivating Docility: A Practical Guide
Chapter II: Crafting a Great Lecture
Chapter III: Leading a Discussion on Poetry
Chapter IV: Cultivating the Memory
Chapter V: Staging a Play
Chapter VI: Assignments, Projects, and Activities from Medieval to Baroque Education
Chapter VII: Further Reading and Resources
Conclusion to Volume II

Volume III: The Enlightenment and Modern Renewal (pairing with *The Heart of Culture*, Chapters Seven–Eleven)
Introduction to Volume III
Part 1: Reflections
Chapter I: The Enlightenment
Chapter II: Renewal in the United States
Chapter III: A Reflection on Integrity
Part 2: The Workbook
Chapter I: Cultivating Integration: A Practical Guide
Chapter II: Leading a Seminar on a Text
Chapter III: Leading a Discussion on Art
Chapter IV: Recommendations for Grading and Assessment
Chapter V: Models of Renewal
Chapter VI: Further Reading and Resources
Conclusion to the Series: Advice from Leaders of Renewal

During the writing of these volumes, I had a chance to interview people actively engaged in the renewal of Catholic education.

Volume I: *Paideia to Monastic Education*

MICHAEL NAUGHTON is the director of the Center for Catholic Studies at the University of St. Thomas (St. Paul, Minnesota) where he holds the Koch Chair in Catholic Studies. His most recent book is *What We Hold in Trust: Rediscovering the Purpose of Catholic Higher Education* (2021).

EMILY DAHDAH is the Director of Educational Quality and Excellence for the Archdiocese of St. Paul, Minnesota. She regularly teaches "Challenges in Catholic PreK–12 Education" for the Department of Catholic Studies at the University of St. Thomas (St. Paul, Minnesota).

RAYMOND HAIN is an Associate Professor of Philosophy and Humanities and Associate Director of the Humanities Program, home of the Catholic Studies major at Providence College (Providence, Rhode Island). He serves on the board of Catholic Studies in Rome, Inc., and the steering committee for the Catholic Studies Consortium.

FR. THOMAS HAAN is the pastor of St. Louis de Montfort (Fishers, Indiana), a parish with a PreK–8 school. Before this, he taught and served as chaplain at St. Theodore Guerin High School (Noblesville, Indiana).

DALE AHLQUIST is the president of the Society of Gilbert Keith Chesterton. He co-founded Chesterton Academy (Hopkins, Minnesota) and serves as president of the Chesterton Schools Network.

CHRISTOPHER FISHER is the Superintendent of the Department of Catholic Schools for the Archdiocese of San Francisco, California. Before this, he served as Executive Director of the Portsmouth Institute for Faith and Culture and teacher at Portsmouth Abbey School (Portsmouth, Rhode Island).

ELISABETH SULLIVAN is the Executive Director of the Institute for Catholic Liberal Education. She has served on Catholic school boards, taught writing and literature, and served as director of communications for a liberal arts school in the Catholic tradition.

CHRISTOPHER BLUM has served at the Augustine Institute (Florissant, Missouri) for over a decade, first as Academic Dean and then as Provost. Before this, he taught at Christendom College (Front Royal, Virginia) and Thomas More College (Merrimack, New Hampshire).

ANDREW SEELEY is Director of Advanced Formation for Educators at the Augustine Institute (Florissant, Missouri), a tutor at Thomas Aquinas College (Santa Paula, California), and co-founder of the Institute for Catholic Liberal Education.

Emily Dahdah observed that "the Church has a great tradition of helping us understand who we are and what we're made for." This tradition helps children learn their identity as sons and daughters of God made to share eternal life with him. If Dahdah were to add anything to *The Heart of Culture*, it would be to emphasize even more strongly that "there's been a substantial rupture with the tradition. Today, many people are struggling to stay close to their roots." Thus, the challenge is to "regraft" them onto the tradition. Given "the severity of our situation," it always encourages Dahdah to visit a great school and see "a new generation regrafted." While the challenges are great, it is a hopeful time for Catholic education. "We're in a renaissance," said Michael Naughton, explaining that every renewal effort, every renaissance starts out this way. First, it recognizes the problems. Then it

Volume I: *Paideia to Monastic Education*

looks to the past. And finally, it draws from that past to create something new.

The Heart of Culture has played a part in the renewal of Catholic education and in the larger drama of salvation. From that text, these volumes take their cue. As did *The Heart of Culture*, these volumes reflect on the problems and look back. Like *The Heart of Culture*, these volumes aim beyond curating and cataloguing the interesting, if outmoded practices of the past. Rather, these volumes draw on the tradition for ideas that have perennial merit and adaptability. Insights from educational leaders like Naughton, Dahdah, and others will conclude these volumes to guide and inspire parents, families, neighborhoods, priests, religious, teachers, professors, pastors, school leaders, superintendents, parishes, and dioceses. This volume now begins the series with an exploration of the roots of Catholic education in Greek *paideia* and the faith of Israel.

CONTENTS

Volume I: *Paideia to Monastic Education*

ACKNOWLEDGMENTS   1

INTRODUCTION TO THE SERIES   3

Part One: Reflections

CHAPTER I: Israel and Greek Paideia   15
   A. *Introduction: The Love of Learning and the Desire for God*   15
   B. *Jewish Education in the Ancient World*   16
   C. *Hellenistic Education in the Ancient World*   18
   D. *Conclusion*   20

CHAPTER II: Christ, the Early Church, and Monasticism   23
   A. *The Christian Model Synthesizes Hellenistic Paideia and Jewish Education*   23
   B. *Monastic Education*   28
   C. *Manual Labor*   31
   D. *The Liturgy and the Desire for God*   33

CHAPTER III: A Reflection on Sensory-Emotional Formation, Wonder, and Studiousness   37
   A. *Distinguishing Sensory-Emotional Formation from Social-Emotional Learning*   39
   B. *The Importance of Sensory-Emotional Formation*   42
   C. *The Subversion of Emotion*   46
   D. *Obstacles to Emotion*   47
   E. *Wonder, Curiosity, and Studiousness*   51

Part Two: The Workbook

CHAPTER I: Cultivating Wonder: A Practical Guide to Sensory-Emotional Formation   59
   A. *Remove Obstacles to the Cultivation of Senses and Emotions*   60
   B. *Offer Experiences That Inspire Wonder*   64
   C. *Reflect*   65
   D. *Make a Plan*   72

CHAPTER II: Physical Education, Song, Dance, and
Manual Labor ... 75
   A. *Physical Education* ... 75
   B. *Singing and Dancing* ... 77
   C. *Manual Labor* ... 78

CHAPTER III: Nature Study and Journaling ... 81
   A. *Goals* ... 82
   B. *Possible Elements of a Single Observation* ... 82
   C. *Process* ... 83
   D. *Ideas for Enriching the Process* ... 85
   E. *Helping Students to Improve Their Observations* ... 92
   F. *A Socratic Discussion about Descriptive Terms* ... 95

CHAPTER IV: Reading Aloud ... 99
   A. *Goals* ... 100
   B. *Preparation* ... 100
   C. *Process* ... 102
   D. *Ideas for for Enriching the Process and Helping Students to Improve Their Reading Aloud* ... 106

CHAPTER V: Leading a Socratic Discussion:
A Variation on Didactic Instruction ... 111
   A. *Goals* ... 112
   B. *Preparation* ... 112
   C. *Process* ... 120
   D. *Other Ideas for Socratic Discussion* ... 122

CHAPTER VI: Assignments, Projects, and Activities
from *Paideia* to Monastic Education ... 125

CHAPTER VII: Further Reading and Resources ... 133

CONCLUSION TO VOLUME I ... 143

PART ONE
Reflections

CHAPTER I

Israel and Greek *Paideia*

A. Introduction: *The Love of Learning and the Desire for God*

The Love of Learning and the Desire for God is the title of Jean Leclercq's work on monastic culture. It is an apt phrase to describe the twin roots of Catholic education: Jewish education and Greek *paideia*. On the one hand, Jewish education is characterized by the desire for God:

> One thing I asked of the LORD,
>   that will I seek after:
> to live in the house of the LORD
>   all the days of my life,
> to behold the beauty of the LORD,
>   and to inquire in his temple (Psalm 27:4, NRSVCE).

On the other hand, Greek *paideia* is characterized by a deep love of learning. The coming of Christ precipitated the marriage of these models, forming a distinctively Catholic form of education, characterized both by the love of learning and the desire for God.

B. *Jewish Education in the Ancient World*

With the guidance of divine inspiration, the Jews set down the story of their relationship with God as it had been revealed to them over many generations. These scripture accounts differed radically from the religious narratives of other traditions. In these accounts, the world was good and created from nothing by a good God, who had a personal and loving relationship with the first human creatures. Disorder came into the world through the Fall, an original sin, which damaged man's relationship with God, self, others, and creation. The story of Israel was one in which God was working to lead his beloved people back to himself. From the first mysterious promise made in Genesis to the covenants and revelations, from Noah and Abraham, to Moses, David, and the prophets, all this was a kind of education.

First, God was imparting information about who he was. Second, God was teaching his people how to worship him in sacrifice. In *The Spirit of the Liturgy*, Joseph Ratzinger reflects on an example from Exodus. God commanded Pharoah to let his people go that they might serve God in the wilderness. Moses wanted to take everyone, including the women. In Pharoah's religious experience, women had no part in worship. He sought a compromise, permitting only the men to go. Moses rejected this and all the other proposed compromises, but not because he understood how to worship God.

Volume I: *Paideia to Monastic Education*

In fact, Moses said as much: "We will not know what to use to worship the Lord until we arrive there" (Exodus 10:26, NRSVCE). Moses had to proceed like a young student, in trusting docility until God instructed him on Mount Sinai about how the people of Israel should worship God. With God as teacher, Israel grew in her understanding of who God is and how to worship him.

Israel's divine education directly influenced her educational focus on the scriptures and divine worship. In the ancient world, the goal of Jewish education was religious observance and fidelity to the Lord. According to Nathan Drazin, "no worldly use was permitted of the 'crown of the Torah.' Even the pursuit of studies for the purpose of obtaining a title like Sage, Rabbi, or elder, or some other honor was highly reprehensible."[1]

Content focused on reading the Torah. Students learned to read aloud. They became familiar with Hebrew. Some learned to write. The education of children took place in the home. Fathers were responsible for educating their sons. Private tutors were rare, although children might receive additional instruction at the house of a teacher, study house, or local synagogue, and, after 64 BC, were expected to do so when possible. By that time, there had been a rise not only in schools for higher learning and secondary schools for adolescents, but a strong interest in the universal education of boys beginning around the age of six or seven. Older students might go on to study under a rabbi. They moved from a

---

1. Nathan Drazin, *History of Jewish Education from 515 BCE to 220 CE* (Baltimore: Johns Hopkins Press, 1940), 22.

focus on the Torah to mastering the rabbi's teaching through memorization and recitation. Like their Greek counterparts, rabbinic schools employed a "face-to-face, personal mode of instruction and discipleship."[2]

The Christians would have to examine whether Jewish education could be harmonized with Greek *paideia*. Was there anything good in *paideia*? What were the hallmarks of this model?

C. Hellenistic Education in the Ancient World

As Christopher Dawson observes, religion is the foundation of every great civilization and the source of its vitality. Greece (and later, Rome) enjoyed this deep connection between religion and culture. For example, the oldest surviving Greek and Roman dramas are associated with religious festivals. And although some of the greatest writers like Plato and Aristotle betray disillusion with the religious cults of the day, they are not irreligious. In fact, their disenchantment with religious cults stems from their devotion to seeking a god who is almighty, all-good, and all-knowing. In the best of Greek culture, there is a deep love of learning and a desire to achieve full human excellence or *areté*.

The Heart of Culture explores the concept of *areté*. The Greek educational model was directed toward cultivating

---

2. Hayim Lapin, "Jewish and Christian Academies in Roman Palestine: Some Preliminary Observations," in *Caesarea Maritima: A Retrospective After Two Millennia*, edited by Avner Raban and Kenneth G. Holum (Leiden: Brill, 1996), 507.

areté in the young, integrating and harmonizing the different aspects of human nature: mind, spirit or emotions, and body. As the concept of *areté* developed, so did the means for achieving it. *Paideia* developed from the two strands of the *trivium* and *quadrivium* into the seven liberal arts. Around age seven to eleven, the earlier stages of *paideia* included gymnastic or physical education, followed by music and poetry. Gymnastic included sports, games, and, for a time, dance. In the *Laws*, the Athenian observes that young people seem unable to sit or be silent; they love to run around and yell. But rhythm and harmony can set this to rights. So the Athenian suggests that the well-educated man should be able to sing and dance well, with good songs and good dances.[3]

Content also included arithmetic, reading, and writing. Students began by reading Homer. A well-prepared reading of a passage was an essential element of the education. To read aloud well and accurately from Homer and other poets was a key goal as well as to recite from memory.

Around age eleven to thirteen, students would proceed to grammatical instruction where they would study the elements of speech and meter. As *paideia* developed, students might continue from grammar to the rest of the seven liberal arts. Education of the young typically took place within the family, usually with the father. Other relatives sometimes helped as did the pedagogue or slave tutor-supervisor,

---

3. Plato, *Laws*, translated by Trevor J. Saunders, in *Plato: Complete Works*, edited with an introduction and notes by John M. Cooper and associate editor D. S. Hutchinson (Indianapolis: Hackett, 1992), II, 653c6–654c2.

especially on the elementary level. Private tutors were more typical of wealthy households.

Paideia was practiced with different emphases in different parts of the world and went through numerous developments and revisions. Eventually Greek influence extended beyond Greece to many other parts of the world and her Hellenistic education was adopted by the Roman Empire.

D. *Conclusion*

As excellent as it was, Hellenistic *paideia* had two weaknesses. First, *paideia* was not informed by revelation about the one, true God and the possibility of resurrection and eternal life. Hellenistic culture was not immune to despair. A verse of the poet Horace suggests that we are "hopeless of return."[4] An ancient Roman tombstone bears the epitaph *In nihil ab nihilo quam cito recidimus*: How quickly we fall back from nothing to nothing. Citing these words, Benedict XVI reflects, "Notwithstanding their gods, they were 'without God' and consequently found themselves in a dark world, facing a dark future" (*Spe Salvi*, §2). It is hard to persevere in education and in life without confidence in a personal and loving God who calls us to eternal life. According to Dawson, "from the time of Plato, the Hellenic *paideia* was a humanism in search for a theology, and the religious tradi-

---

4. Horace, "Book 2, Ode 3," in *The Odes and Carmen Saeculare of Horace*, translated by John Conington (London: George Bell and Sons, 1882).

tions of Greek culture were neither deep nor wide enough to provide the answer."[5]

Second, *paideia* lacked the assistance of sanctifying grace. While there is much to applaud in Hellenistic culture, there is also much to deplore. The Hellenistic world was a world in need of grace. The greatness encompassed in *areté* was hard to achieve. According to Thomas Merton, the Greek tragedies explore why even the greatest men fall. What is source of this wound? Is there any remedy?[6] Far from thinking that man would evolve to some nobler and better state, people began to question if man was fundamentally, perhaps hopelessly flawed.

Any educational model would be improved by the influence of *paideia* and the Greek ideal of *areté*. But that influence is not enough. Educational models need grace. They need God.

---

5. Christopher Dawson, "The Origins of the Western Tradition of Education," in *The Crisis of Western Education* (New York: Sheed and Ward, 1961), 8.
6. Thomas Merton, "Greek Tragedy: Suffering Leads to Wisdom," audio recording of a lecture at the Abbey of Gethsemane, Trappist, Kentucky, August 1965 (via *Learn25*, 2018).

CHAPTER II

Christ, the Early Church, and Monasticism

A. The Christian Model Synthesizes Hellenistic Paideia and Jewish Education

Jesus Christ gives meaning to everything and his coming has implications for everything. In the context of education, the coming of Christ led Christians to synthesize Hellenistic *paideia* and Jewish education. The end of chapter two in *The Heart of Culture* reflects on seven key elements of *paideia*. This section revisits these elements in light of the Christian model, which adopted and elevated the best of *paideia* while resolving its weaknesses.

First: Christians adopted something like *areté* while expanding the concept of human excellence. To virtues that the Greeks had recognized by the aid of reason alone was added an understanding of faith, hope, and charity, a call to put on Christ and become partakers of God's divine nature. Further, Christians received new impetus for excellence. In the face of death, *areté* sometimes lacked the power to inspire its pursuit. Christ's resurrection, the possibility of eternal life, and the restoration of mankind to a relationship with God gave new meaning and motivation for human efforts. No effort was wasted; everything could be offered as a form of prayer and preparation for eternal life.

Second and third: Christians also assumed a specific human anthropology. To the Greek anthropology was added the understanding that we are made in the image and likeness of God, as well as clarity about the weakness of fallen human nature. Christians adopted the Hellenistic interest in studying the true, good, and beautiful, regardless of whether such study provided career advancement. They also aimed to form a certain kind of person, one enjoying integrity of mind and body, inner life and outer behavior. But now there was the assistance of sacramental grace. It still might be hard to achieve certain aspects of *areté*, such as physical strength or intellectual ability, but sacramental grace made it universally possible to achieve excellence of character and to a degree of perfection hitherto unimaginable. Consider the great variety of saints, from every walk of life and living out the virtues that the Greeks had most admired.

Fourth and sixth: Christians adopted the desire for truth and belief in the ability of the mind to find it. They adopted and developed the seven liberal arts as well as Hellenistic epistemology to shape their own pedagogical practices.

Fifth and seventh: Teaching became a form of charity. At its best, Hellenistic *paideia* was relational and personal, taking place in the context of a community of learners. Think of Socrates' relationship with Plato or Xenophon or Plato's relationship with Aristotle. A good student-teacher relationship was based on natural loves like family love and friendship. However, the experience did not always live up to the standard. Augustine (354–430) writes about experiences with difficult teachers in his pagan Hellenistic education. As a teacher, he experienced many problems in the educational culture and came to loath his students in Carthage and Rome.

Jewish education also employed a personal mode. Jesus had used this with his own apostles, a group of disciples learning from a teacher who taught face-to-face and by personal example. In the footsteps of Jesus, Christian educators added charity to these existing personal modes of instruction, extending the love of Christ to every student. Those students would learn in the context of community. They would grow into men and women who shared what they had received with the next generation of students. For example, Robert L. Wilken writes how Origen (c. 185–253) "sought to change the lives of his students by establishing a personal and intimate relation with them."[1] While Augustine writes of poor student-teacher relationships, he also notes a very different experience. This was the formative influence of Ambrose (c. 340–397), a Christian, a bishop with the charism of teaching. Augustine remembers: "I came to love him, not at first as a teacher of the truth, which I had utterly despaired of finding in Your Church, but for his kindness towards me."[2] This marriage of pedagogy with charity came to characterize the work of Catholic education.

---

1. Robert L. Wilken, "Alexandria: A School for Training in Virtue," in *Schools of Thought in the Christian Tradition*, edited by Patrick Henry (Philadelphia: Fortress, 1984), 21.
2. Augustine, *Confessions*, translated by Frank Sheed (Indianapolis: Hackett, 1993), V.13.

Christians also adopted the Jewish educational emphasis on directing all studies toward the worship of God. Basil (330–379) was a bishop, prolific author, the founder of numerous Christian communities, and a father of the Church who influenced early monasticism. He addressed the Christian attitude to Hellenistic *paideia* and culture in his "Address to Young Men on How They Might Derive Benefit from Greek Literature." Here he writes that "a contest, the greatest of all contests, lies before us, for which we must do all things, and, in preparation for it, must strive to the best of our power, and must associate with poets and writers of prose and orators and with all men from whom there is any prospect of benefit with reference to the care of our soul."[3]

A monastic exercise would interrogate a work with this question: How is this useful? But this question was different from the contemporary: How are we going to use this? When a student asks this today, he often means: How is this going to help me find a job or achieve earthly success? To the contrary, the monastic question meant: How will this draw me closer to God? In *On Christian Teaching*, Augustine notes that only God himself can be understood as something to enjoy for "its own sake." We enjoy and explore his creation rightly when we do so with reference to him. Ultimately, Christians study the world for the sake of loving God and making him known and loved. The Christian model borrowed elements that could aid evangelization and

---

3. Basil, "Address to Young Men on How They Might Derive Benefit from Greek Literature," translated by Roy J. Defarrari, in *St. Basil: The Letters*, translated by Roy J. Defarrari and Martin R. P. McGuire, vol. 4 (Cambridge: Harvard University Press, 1950), 1–2.

the formation of new followers of Christ, from language to philosophical categories to poetry. Early Christian educators were interested in more than teaching information and skills. They were interested in a full transformation, a conversion of character.

The desire to study the true, good, and beautiful for the sake of the One who is Truth, Goodness, and Beauty led to a Christian educational synthesis of the two traditions, a model with room for variation. For example, one early Christian model started with the study of logic, followed with natural history, geometry, astronomy, ethics, theological and philosophical writings, and culminated in the study of scripture, while other models included more scripture or began scripture study earlier in the sequence. The Monastic era (c. 300–1100) focused on grammar and textual study. The students at these schools were primarily clerics and future religious. The Medieval era (c. 1000–1400) focused on logic and analysis. The students at cathedral schools and universities were primarily clerics and future religious, but more laity were represented. The Renaissance and Baroque era (c. 1400–1700) focused on rhetoric and expression via language studies, writing, art, theater, and debate. In this era, the Jesuit order played a key part in shaping educational models and founding institutions open to laity, clergy, and future religious. Although each period may have focused on one aspect of the *trivium*, the whole *trivium* was studied throughout these centuries. A smaller percentage of students continued their studies beyond the *trivium* to study the *quadrivium*. In different ways, each period engaged with, borrowed from, and baptized the best elements of Hellenistic culture as well as elements from new cultures encountered in the centuries after Christ.

After the Enlightenment (c. late 1600s–1815), Catholic education saw efforts to restore what had nearly been destroyed by revolution, new religious teaching orders and lay initiatives dedicated to the mission of Catholic education, and new forms of Catholic educational renewal.

B. *Monastic Education*

Between the fourth and sixth centuries, Christians saw the rise of eastern and western monastic communities. They followed different rules, for example, one composed by Augustine, another by Basil. *The Rule of St. Benedict* enjoyed a slow dissemination, achieving widespread influence during the Carolingian Renaissance.

Chapter four in *The Heart of Culture* explains how monastic schools developed. In *The Love of Learning and the Desire for God,* Jean Leclercq observes that a monastic school looked partly like a Jewish school with its focus on the scriptures, and partly like a Hellenistic school with its training in grammar. Monastic education also featured the ongoing dual appreciation for and suspicion of pagan authors. Monks both disparaged pagan authors and sought to mine the good in their texts. Teaching remained face-to-face and personal. It was not uncommon for teachers to select talented or committed students for additional training.

In a monastic educational establishment, some monks learned how to keep accounts. But primarily, a monastic

Volume I: *Paideia to Monastic Education*

educational establishment focused on grammar. That is, it taught the following:

- Reading, which included reading comprehension and the ability to read aloud in a meditative fashion, savoring and ruminating on the words with the participation of body, memory, intelligence, and will. The three areas of reading were Scripture, the Fathers, and classical literature. The fathers included both Greek and Latin authors. Classical literature included everything from natural history and poetry to philosophy.
- Writing, which was taught to assist copying and study. Monastic schools did not teach or give assignments in literary genres. But monastic education led many to engage freely in various forms of writing including history, hagiography, sermons, letters, and *florilegia*. Like a commonplace book, the *florilegium* was a compilation of favorite excerpts and quotations from one's reading, often addressing a particular topic or theme and beautifully illuminated.

Various pedagogical methods were employed, for example:

- Preparing an "Accessus ad auctores," a short reflection on a work.
- Written commentary or explanation of the texts, for example, a literary gloss or annotation explaining words and phrases.
- Oral commentaries delivered on the meaning of a text, from discussions on individual words to the

whole text. Commentaries could include tools like declining or conjugating words and the equivalent of sentence diagramming.
- Copying, which included bookbinding, calligraphy, papermaking, and the equivalent of preparing a critical edition by editing, commenting, and comparing various versions or translations of a work.

Although the emphasis was on the grammar aspect of the *trivium*, the influence of the *quadrivium* was everywhere, from Gregorian chant to the design of churches and monasteries. Stratford Caldecott suggests that the third component of the *quadrivium* (music) can be understood more broadly to include aspects of Greek "musical" education like song, story, poetry, and dance or gymnastic. In this sense, monastic communities incarnated the *quadrivium* through the orderliness of their life, which was "proportionate, harmonious, disciplined, and (often) joyful."[4]

The monastic model of education fostered other aspects of formation besides proficiency in reading and writing. First, its students developed their understanding of Catholic theology. Second, its students developed powerful memories and lively imaginations. Leclercq writes how these well-trained imaginations "permitted them to picture…the colors and dimensions of things, the clothing, bearing, and actions of the

---

4. Stratford Caldecott, "Educating the Poetic Imagination," in *Beauty for Truth's Sake: The Re-Enchantment of Education* (Grand Rapids, MI: Brazos Press, 2009), 39.

people, the complex environment in which they move. They liked to describe them and, so to speak, re-create them, giving very sharp relief to images and feelings."[5] Finally, its students developed a fully integrated contemplative receptivity. Habits like reading aloud provided tactile and aural memory as well as visual memory of words. Whether an individual was reading to himself or listening to a text read aloud to a group, he was engaged physically, emotionally, and mentally. Because the education tended to engage the whole person, it had a powerful influence on the ability of the monks to give their attention fully and deeply to the created order and to God.

This literary education took place within a wider monastic culture characterized by two other elements. The first element was manual labor. The second element was the liturgy, through which the monks encountered the source and goal of monastic culture and education.

C. Manual Labor

The early Christians included manual laborers, artisans, and even slaves, for example, Onesimus, who is named in Paul's letter to Philemon. From that time, Christians developed a theology of work rooted in the scriptures and developed in the writings of fathers and doctors of the Church all the way to the documents of the Second Vatican Council and

---

5. Jean Leclercq, *The Love of Learning and the Desire for God: A Study of Monastic Culture*, 3rd ed., translated by Catharine Misraki (New York: Fordham University, 2001), 75.

the encyclicals of Pope Francis. Manual labor was a key element of *The Rule of St. Benedict* and monastic culture. For Christians, work can be offered as a form of prayer and praise. It reminds one of the importance of perseverance in the spiritual life. It is a remedy for idleness and its spiritual dangers. It supports the community. It develops human gifts. While toil is a result of the Fall, work is a gift from God that predates the Fall. Through work, man imitates God the creator.

In *Laborem Exercens*, John Paul II observes that Jesus who "became like us in all things devoted most of the years of his life on earth to manual work at the carpenter's bench" (section 6, §5). Work has a power to foster communion. This includes our grateful relationship to God the creator and sustainer of all that makes life and work possible. It includes those who came before us and developed the tools and knowledge we use to work. It includes our fellow human beings and those who will come after us, most especially those who benefit directly from our labor and service. And it includes our families and children. John Paul II writes, "The family is simultaneously a community made possible by work and the first school of work, within the home, for every person" (section 10, §2).

This theology of work appeared in many elements of monastic life. Many monastic rules made room for members of the community to develop their gifts and talents. Many monastic communities saw their work as one in communion with God, imitating and cooperating with his salvific work. Building churches and shrines, keeping hospitality, digging wells, and maintaining irrigation systems were works that signified the coming kingdom.

Volume I: *Paideia to Monastic Education*

We can learn from the harmonious way monastic culture placed formal education and the study of the liberal arts within a broader context that respected and practiced manual arts. We can provide students with opportunities to learn how to offer their toil, develop their gifts, serve their fellow man, and cooperate with God in extending his creative and saving work.

D. *The Liturgy and the Desire for God*

The Rule of St. Benedict outlined how its monks would pause seven times during the day and once during the night to praise the Lord. Monastic communities built their calendar around feasts of the Church and used what they learned to celebrate these feasts. As Leclercq writes in a chapter beautifully titled "The Poem of the Liturgy": "The monks' entire life was led under the sign of the liturgy, in rhythm with its hours, its seasons, and its feasts; it was dominated by the desire to glorify God in everything, and first of all, by celebrating His mysteries."[6] George Ovitt observes that the purpose of labor "was the creation of both a physical and spiritual context within which God could be more fully worshiped."[7] Similarly, Leclercq writes that the purpose of study "was intended to teach the monks and the clerics the right way to live, and at the same time how to speak well and write well in order to

---

6. Leclercq, *The Love of Learning and the Desire for God*, 237.
7. George Ovitt, "The Cultural Context of Western Technology: Early Christian Attitudes toward Manual Labor," in *Technology and Culture* 27, no. 3 (1986): 499.

pray well."[8] From reading to digging, monastic culture and education were ordered to the liturgy and the worship of God.

Monastic culture and education had far-reaching effects. As *The Heart of Culture* relates, monastic schools produced numerous leaders of the Middle Ages: educational leaders, founders of religious orders, and counselors to kings and emperors. The creative output of monastic communities is astounding. Consider their agricultural, engineering, and technological advances: draining swamps, building mills and reservoirs, metalworking, and innovations in liqueurs, beer brewing, and winemaking. They built farms, orchards, libraries, and infirmaries. Consider the many illuminations, the development of musical notation, and the composition of hymns such as the Easter Sequence or the *Veni Creator Spiritus*, which is still a feature of the rite of profession for religious vows and the ordination of a deacon, priest, or bishop. John Henry Newman reflects:

> Silent men were observed about the country, or discovered in the forest, digging, clearing, and building; and other silent men, not seen, were sitting in the cold cloister, tiring their eyes, and keeping their attention on the stretch, while they painfully deciphered and copied and re-copied the manuscripts which they had saved.... By degrees the woody swamp became a hermitage, a religious

---

8. Leclercq, *The Love of Learning and the Desire for God*, 244.

house, a farm, an abbey, a village, a seminary, a school of learning, and a city.[9]

And yet, monastic culture and education were directed beyond these goods. As Leclercq observes, the monks were neither collectors, curators, nor aesthetes.[10] They had not embraced monastic life "for any practical or social end."[11] Monastic culture and education were fueled by one thing: the desire for God.

---

9. John Henry Newman, "The Mission of St. Benedict," in *Historical Sketches*, vol. 2 (London: Longmans, Green, & Company, 1906), 410.
10. Leclercq, *The Love of Learning and the Desire for God*, 134.
11. Ibid., 18–19.

CHAPTER III

A Reflection on Sensory-Emotional Formation, Wonder, and Studiousness

CATHOLIC EDUCATION borrowed and developed an epistemology that recognized how intellectual and spiritual formation build on sensory-emotional formation. This chapter reflects on this foundation with particular attention to the emotion of wonder and the virtue of studiousness.

Sensory-emotional formation exercises the five exterior senses (sight, hearing, touch, smell, and taste). It exercises the four interior senses (common, imaginative, memorative, and estimative), affording opportunities for the common sense to distinguish, imagination to imagine, memory to remember, and the estimative sense to encounter good things as good and bad things as bad. It continues by eliciting proper emotional responses. As we develop in years and experience, intellectual and spiritual formation build on sensory-emotional formation.

We are wounded by the Fall. Our intellects are darkened, and our wills inclined to sin. To become who God made us to be, it helps to participate in the sacramental life of the Catholic Church, especially through participation in the Holy Sacrifice of the Mass and regular Confession. It helps to learn about the role of virtue in human flourishing and achieving our final end in God. Appropriate punishments and rewards are also helpful. Intellectual and spiritual formation can offer all this assistance.

But, after the sacraments, perhaps most helpful is a sensory-rich, emotionally powerful experience in which we witness someone suffering the disfigurement of vice or, even better, doing the good in a beautiful way. These experiences illuminate intellectual explanations and motivate the will. We can offer such experiences to the young. We can practice virtue and share personal stories. We can share experiences from history, lives of the saints, literature, and works of art. To read and discuss *The Lion, the Witch, and the Wardrobe* with a child in a manner which involves his senses and provides room for a proper emotional response to the hard and beautiful events of the book—that is sensory-emotional formation.

Here is why it matters. How does a child begin to overcome a vice, for example, greed? Participation in the Mass and regular Confession offer grace to overcome temptation, provided he has the required disposition.[1] He might listen to an explanation about the merits of temperance. He might obey a rule to avoid punishment or earn a reward. But another powerful influence might be the strong imaginative memory of a cold white winter in Narnia, with jingling bells and Edmund Pevensie stuffing himself with the evil queen's Turkish Delight. What can inspire someone to curb his greed or regulate an emotion out of control so powerfully as another

---

1. *Catechism of the Catholic Church*, 2nd ed. (Vatican City: Vatican Press, 1997), 1128, 1131.

rightly ordered emotion: disgust at Edmund's greed, sorrow for his treachery, love of Aslan, joy at Edmund's repentance and redemption? Grounded in rich sensory details, embedded in imagination and memory, these proper emotional responses to the deeds of Edmund and Aslan dispose a child to recognize greed for what it is and *want* the grace, the intellectual explanations, and the communal support to help him practice temperance. Thus, sensory-emotional formation lays the foundation for intellectual and spiritual formation. Those later forms of formation never stop using the senses and emotions to inspire the intellect, motivate the will, and order the senses and emotions, taking them "up into the virtues," so that the human person loves God with his whole heart, soul, mind, and strength.[2]

A. *Distinguishing Sensory-Emotional Formation from Social-Emotional Learning*

Before I go into more detail, I want to distinguish sensory-emotional formation from Social-Emotional Learning. Sensory-emotional formation forms five physical senses, four interior senses, and the full range of human emotions in non-didactic, informal, ongoing, and experiential ways. Social-Emotional Learning teaches five competencies: self-awareness, social awareness, self-management, relationship skills, and responsible decision-making. Because Social-Emotional Learning has become a regular feature in many

---

2. Ibid., 1768. See also Mark 12:30, NRSVCE.

education programs, it may be helpful to explore the distinction. The phrases sound similar and both are connected to education. There are several differences between sensory-emotional formation and Social-Emotional Learning. The first difference is theological while the second concerns content and pedagogy.

First, sensory-emotional formation can be traced to the Greeks and Christians who adopted and baptized the formation. It assumes a Christian telos and anthropology. Although some argue that Social-Emotional Learning can also be traced to the Greeks, its immediate origin dates to the late twentieth century. Most Social-Emotional Learning programs have a secular worldview. Aquinas College and the Institute for the Transformation of Catholic Education have been developing a Catholic Social-Emotional Learning program to overcome this theological difference. Integration with Catholic theology would have a clear impact on the five competencies: self-awareness, social awareness, self-management, relationship skills, and responsible decision-making. A Catholic Social-Emotional Learning program would recognize the unity of body and soul and our identity as children of God, made for God. It would admit our fallen nature and our need for Jesus Christ who became a man, suffered, died, rose, and instituted the Catholic Church as his body to preserve divine revelation and the means of salvation. It would aim beyond managing emotions toward harmonizing emotions with intellect and will toward the love of God. It would aim beyond relationship skills toward the practice of divine charity. It would aim beyond responsible decision-making toward the quest for eternal life. Integration with Catholic theology would elevate the telos of most Social-Emotional Learning programs.

However, a Catholic Social-Emotional Learning program would still differ from sensory-emotional formation in terms of pedagogy and content. First, sensory-emotional formation does not come through discrete didactic lessons but instead is informal, ongoing, and experiential. Sensory-emotional formation works best when it shapes a culture. For every individual assent to a single truth and every individual virtuous deed, there are a hundred sensory-emotional experiences which testify to the veracity of that truth and the efficacy of that virtuous deed in the quest for God. Sensory-emotional formation provides the raw data which intellectual and spiritual formation use to do their work. Second, sensory-emotional formation does not teach three Social-Emotional Learning competencies: self-management, relationships skills, or responsible decision-making. Finally, sensory-emotional formation goes beyond awareness of self-awareness and social awareness, beyond awareness of bodily states and emotions to a more explicit cultivation of the five physical senses, four interior senses, and the full range of human emotions. However, in this process, people do tend to become more observant of reality in general, including their own bodily states, emotions, and the needs and characters of other people. Thus, sensory-emotional formation indirectly aids the self-awareness and social awareness competencies of Social-Emotional Formation.

Most Social-Emotional Learning programs do not seem to include sensory-emotional formation. Thus, it seems possible to be the successful product of a Social-Emotional

Learning Program while retaining a poor sensory-emotional formation. This person recognizes states like hunger, anger, and the connection between those states, but lacks awareness of summer scents, poetic rhythm, or variations in the shading of a bird's throat. This person makes responsible decisions and navigates social situations but suffers an impoverished imagination and memory. This person knows how to name and manage the emotions he does experience, but endures a limited emotional range: anger, sadness, and joy are common but gratitude, loyalty, pity, wonder, and magnanimity are rare.

A Social-Emotional Learning program would be improved not only by integration with Catholic theology but also by incorporating sensory-emotional formation. Sensory-emotional formation would extend the pedagogy of Social-Emotional Learning in non-didactic, informal, ongoing, and experiential ways while deepening the content of two competencies of Social-Emotional Learning (self-awareness and social awareness) through formation of the five physical senses, four interior senses, and the full range of human emotions.

Now, on to a closer look at sensory-emotional formation, wonder, curiosity, and studiousness.

B. *The Importance of Sensory-Emotional Formation*

Human learning starts with well-developed senses. Aristotle stresses an order to the development of human faculties. Aquinas echoes this: "The action of one depends on another."[3] The five exterior senses include sight, hearing, touch, smell, and taste. The four interior senses include imagination and memory, as well as the common and estimative sense. The common sense enables us to distinguish between sense perceptions, for example, between something we see and something we smell. Like instinct in animals, the estimative sense enables us to sense when something is likely to help or hinder our flourishing. We are also creatures with emotions which influence and are influenced by the body and the soul. It is difficult to apprehend and choose the good without well-developed emotions. Sensory-emotional formation cultivates the five exterior senses and the four interior senses. It also cultivates the full range of human emotions, teaching and modeling virtue to harmonize those emotions with the intellect and will in pursuit of the good.

In *The Laws*, Plato has the Athenian compare sensory-emotional formation with intellectual formation. Who is better educated? The man with intellectual formation but no sensory-emotional formation? Or the man with sensory-emotional formation but no intellectual formation?

> THE ATHENIAN: Now then, take a man whose opinion about what is good is correct (it really is good), and likewise in the case of the bad (it really is bad), and follows this judgement in practice. He

---

3. Thomas Aquinas, *Summa Theologiae*, 2nd ed., translated by the Fathers of the English Dominican Province, 1920, I, q. 77, a. 4, ad 3. See also I, q. 77, a. 4, body; I, q. 85, art. 7, body; I-II, q. 64, a. 4; II-II, q. 35, a. 3 and 4; II-II, q. 166, a. 2; II-II, q. 167, a. 1 and 2.

> may be able to represent, by word and gesture, and with invariable success, his intellectual conception of what is good, even though he gets no pleasure from it and feels no hatred for what is bad. Another man may not be very good at keeping on the right lines when he uses his body and his voice to represent the good, or at trying to form some intellectual conception of it; but he may be very much on the right lines in his feelings of pleasure and pain, because he welcomes what is good and loathes what is bad. Which of these two will be the better educated musically, and the more effective member of a chorus?
>
> CLINIAS: As far as education is concerned, sir, the second is infinitely superior.[4]

Plato seems to suggest that, if one had to choose between intellectual and sensory-emotional formation, it would be better to choose the second. In Plato's *Republic*, Socrates praises the outcome of sensory-emotional formation:

> Since he has the right distastes, he'll praise fine things, be pleased by them, receive them into his soul, and, being nurtured by them, become fine and good. He'll rightly object to what is shameful, hating it while he's still young and unable to grasp the reason, but, having been educated in this way, he will welcome the reason when it comes

---

4. Plato, *Laws*, II, 654c4–d8.

and recognize it easily because of its kinship with himself.[5]

With a good sensory-emotional formation, a person will more easily recognize truth, goodness, or beauty because he will have a taste for those things. He will more easily accept intellectual arguments about the good because the arguments will resonate on a deep level. Finally, he will more easily choose the good and avoid evil because he has the help of well-formed emotions. As Aristotle explains in the *Nicomachean Ethics*, "Men choose what is pleasant and avoid what is painful."[6]

Certainly, it is admirable to choose the good despite emotions pulling for the contrary. However, God wants us to enjoy interior harmony. And according to Aquinas, a good act is made better when it is motivated not only by intellect and will but also by rightly ordered emotion.[7] In practice, it is quite hard to choose the good in opposition to emotion. C. S. Lewis even suggests that "without the aid of trained emotions the intellect is powerless against the animal organism."[8]

---

5. Plato, *Republic*, 2nd ed., translated by G. M. A. Grube, revised by C. D. C. Reeve (Indianapolis: Hackett, 1992), III, 401e3–402a4.
6. Aristotle, *Ethics*, in *The Basic Works of Aristotle*, edited with an introduction by Richard McKeon (New York: Random House, 1941), X.1, 1172a25–26.
7. Thomas Aquinas, *Summa Theologiae*, I-II, q. 24, a. 3, body and ad 1.
8. C. S. Lewis, *The Abolition of Man* (New York: Collier Books, 1962), 33.

C. The Subversion of Emotion

If we ignore sensory-emotional formation, we will have less success trying to lead people to truth, goodness, and beauty. Moreover, if other influences conspire to subvert senses and emotions, the task will be even harder. Subversion is chillingly depicted in C. S. Lewis' *That Hideous Strength*. The novel relates the story of the newly married couple Jane and Mark Studdock. Mark Studdock is exploring a new position with the National Institute of Co-ordinated Experiments (N.I.C.E). Mark slowly becomes aware of an inner circle of leaders who serve the Macrobes. Mark is not sure what the Macrobes are. As the story progresses, readers get hints that the Macrobes are demonic powers.

When the leaders at N.I.C.E. decide to initiate Mark into the inner circle and the service of the Macrobes, they commence a peculiar form of education. It begins in a misshapen room covered in random dots and decorated with strange pictures. The pictures feature disturbing details such as a man with corkscrews for arms, a woman with fur on her tongue, and a Last Supper scene swarming with insects. Later, the educational exercises ask Mark to engage in obscenities and eventually to trample a crucifix. Mark is not Christian. But he soon grasps that the point is to undergo an education that will prepare him for the demonic society of the organization's leaders. Repeated exposure in a clinical, supposedly amoral environment is aimed at neutralizing and transforming all of Mark's gut reactions, from his estimative sense to his emotions. However, Mark reacts in an unexpected way. He gets a feeling for something connected to the love of his wife, fried eggs, soap, sunlight, birds, and daylight: "He was not thinking in moral terms at all; or else (what is much the same thing) he was having his first deeply moral experience. He was choosing a side: the Normal."[9] How Mark escapes his subversive education is the story of the book.

This kind of subversion goes on all the time. We see it in real and fictional depictions of sin portrayed in funny, sympathetic, or even glamorous ways. Repeated exposure to these kinds of depictions does not provide rational reasons to practice or condone these behaviors. Rather, it dulls senses and disorders emotions. People are no longer pained by things that should pain them, while it becomes a struggle to delight in things that should delight. The longer emotions remain disordered, the harder it is to recognize truth, goodness, and beauty. Most people will act in conformity with disordered emotion and eventually, align their convictions to those emotions. Thus, Aristotle argues that we need "to have been brought up in a particular way from our very youth, as Plato says, so as both to delight in and to be pained by the things that we ought; for this is right education."[10]

D. *Obstacles to Emotion*

However, in some classrooms and congregations, people can seem apathetic or numb. The problem seems less about

---

9. C. S. Lewis, *That Hideous Strength* (New York: MacMillan, 1967), 299.
10. Aristotle, *Ethics*, II.3, 1104b11–13.

strong subverted emotions and more about an apparent lack of emotion. Can we do sensory-emotional formation with people who seem to lack emotion? Yes, we can and in the same way that Catholic education has done it since it first drew on Greek epistemology. However, we may need to make an additional effort to remove potential obstacles to the proper experience of emotion.

One source for the numbing of emotions can be cultural expectations. For example, in *Little Town on the Prairie*, Laura Ingalls Wilder relates a nineteenth-century cultural prohibition against the expression of emotion. She recalls her family's reaction at a church event. They enter and see the beautiful decorations and bountiful table: "Laura stood stock-still for an instant. Even Pa and Ma almost halted, though they were too grown-up to show surprise. A grown-up person must never let feelings be shown by voice or manner. So Laura only looked, and gently hushed Grace, though she was as excited and overwhelmed as Carrie was."[11] Sixty years later, C. S. Lewis published *The Abolition of Man*. In it, he writes that "for every one pupil who needs to be guarded from a weak excess of sensibility there are three who need to be awakened from the slumber of cold vulgarity. The task of the modern educator is not to cut down jungles but to irrigate deserts."[12] Cultural distaste for emotion continues. When there are displays of excessive and riotous emotion, some react by buckling down on stoic indifference.

---

11. Laura Ingalls Wilder, *Little Town on the Prairie* (New York: HarperCollins, 2016), 228.
12. Lewis, *The Abolition of Man*, 24.

Volume I: *Paideia to Monastic Education*

Nevertheless, the Catholic Church has always upheld the goodness of human emotions. Christ himself experienced and showed many emotions: he wept; he marveled. Aquinas comments on the scripture passages that depict Christ experiencing wonder. At first glance, it seems odd that Christ would manifest wonder. As a divine being, he knows everything. But Aquinas explains that Christ "assumed [wonder] for our instruction, i.e. in order to teach us to wonder at what He Himself wondered at."[13] God gave us emotions. When these emotions are in good working order, we should feel them, as Christ did.

A second source for the numbing of emotions can be the surfeit of stimulus. In "Learning How to See Again," Josef Pieper recounts a magnificent sight. One night on board a cruise, he sees hundreds of luminous sea creatures glowing in the dark waters of the Atlantic. The next day he hears people mention that there was nothing to be seen on the previous night. Considering this strange statement, Pieper writes, "The average person of our time loses the ability to see because *there is too much to see!*" Surrounded by "visual noise," senses and emotions grow dull.[14]

A third source for numbing of emotions can be trauma. When people endure intense suffering, they sometimes respond by shutting down emotionally. Auschwitz survivor Victor Frankl describes how the emotion of wonder died in

---

13. Thomas Aquinas, *Summa Theologiae*, III, q. 15, a. 8, body.
14. Josef Pieper, "Learning How to See Again," in *Only the Lover Sings*, translated by Lothar Krauth (San Francisco: Ignatius Press, 1990), 32–33.

the concentration camps. When the men were freed, they found that years apart from beauty, creation, and goodness had made them insensible:

> We came to a meadow full of flowers. We saw and realized that they were there, but we had no feelings about them. The first spark of joy came when we saw a rooster with a tail of multicolored feathers. But it remained only a spark; we did not yet belong to this world.
>
> In the evening when we all met again in our hut, one said secretly to the other, "Tell me, were you pleased today?"
>
> And the other replied, feeling ashamed as he did not know that we all felt similarly, "Truthfully, no!" We had literally lost the ability to feel pleased.[15]

Incredibly, Frankl adds that they could and did slowly relearn their ability to experience emotions like wonder.

We need to be aware that students may be coming from traumatic backgrounds. Research suggests that more than half of American adults have experienced at least one Adverse Childhood Experience, potentially traumatic events that include experiencing or witnessing violence, abuse, neglect, substance abuse, mental health issues, parental separa-

---

15. Viktor E. Frankl, *Man's Search for Meaning: An Introduction to Logotherapy*, 3rd ed., translated by Ilse Lasch, with a preface by Gordon W. Allport (New York: Simon & Schuster, 1984), 95.

tion, incarceration, or the suicide of a family member.[16] We need to work with parents, counselors, religious, and priests to offer experiences of love and peace, so that students can experience natural emotions. We need to moderate the flood of stimuli to the capacities and needs of the young. We need to work against cultural norms condemning emotions. Whether we have one or all three of these influences at work, we can still help in awakening and attuning emotions to truth, goodness, and beauty, so that they harmonize with and serve intellect and will in the search for God.

F. *Wonder, Curiosity, and Studiousness*

The first chapter in the Workbook describes the sensory-emotional formation process in detail. While it could explore many emotions, it focuses on the emotion of wonder for two reasons. First, the practices that cultivate wonder also cultivate the other emotions. To learn how to form wonder is to learn how to do sensory-emotional formation. Second, wonder is an emotion particularly helpful for learning. The emotion of wonder is a gift from God. When we encounter the effect of some unknown cause or see something that sur-

---

16. Melissa T. Merrick, Derek C. Ford, Katie A. Ports, and Angie S. Guinn, "Prevalence of Adverse Childhood Experiences from the 2011–2014 Behavioral Risk Factor Surveillance System in 23 States," *JAMA Pediatrics* 172, no. 11 (2018): 1038–1044, doi:10.1001/jamapediatrics.2018.2537; Zachary Giano, Denna L. Wheeler, and Randolph D. Hubach, "The Frequencies and Disparities of Adverse Childhood Experiences in the U.S.," *BMC Public Health* 20, no. 1 (2020): 1327, doi:10.1186/s12889-020-09411-z.

passes understanding, we experience a thrill. Wonder sparks the desire for understanding, sometimes the beginnings of love, a desire for union with the source of the wonder.

Once wonder awakens, intellectual and spiritual formation can begin to encourage the virtue of studiousness. For without this virtue, wonder can deteriorate into curiosity. For centuries, the Catholic educational tradition has regarded curiosity as a vice. It takes many forms. For example, curiosity seeks to understand things permanently beyond our capacity, such as the mystery of the Trinity. Curiosity seeks forbidden knowledge or seeks for a bad reason, for example, for the sake of lust or to engage in gossip. Curiosity seeks knowledge from forbidden sources, such as demons and astrology.

Curiosity takes another form when it takes us away from studies that are part of our obligations. For example, to serve our family, we might begin to study a particular skill. Curiosity would distract us to pursue other knowledge in a way which robbed us of time, energy, and attention for the skill.

Curiosity takes another form when it takes us away from studies that are more important. Curiosity prizes the trivial over the vital. But the Catholic educational tradition upholds a hierarchy of knowledge. While defending the worth of other disciplines, Newman writes that all disciplines "go to make up one whole, differing only according to their relative importance…. Theology is one branch of knowledge, and Secular Sciences are other branches. Theology is the highest indeed, and widest."[17] A fifteenth-century

---

17. John Henry Newman, "General Knowledge Viewed as One Philosophy," in *Discourses on the Scope and Nature of University Education* (Dublin: James Duffy, 1852), 152.

illuminated manuscript from the Lake Constance area personifies the seven liberal arts as women dressed in gowns of green, red, and white. The women of the *trivium* are pulling a four-wheeled cart. The women of the *quadrivium* each help to a turn a wheel of the cart. Riding in the cart and seated on a cushion is a woman dressed in white and crowned with gold. In her hands she holds up a cloth that looks like part of the Shroud of Turin. The woman is Holy Theology gazing at the face of Christ. Thus, in choosing our study, we must discern our obligations and the relative merits of the object of study.

Finally, curiosity takes another form when we seek to learn without reference to God. True wonder is characterized by increasing attention to and desire for God. But curiosity distracts. For Aquinas, where there is curiosity, there is evidence of a deeper problem: sloth. Sloth is considered a deadly sin because it cultivates distaste for God and spiritual goods. Because we are made for God, sloth can produce a great deal of inner conflict and restlessness. This generates a desire for distraction. Curiosity provides a fix.

Research suggests that wonder produces chemical and physical changes within the body, including the release of dopamine. This primes people to continue searching, swilling information about things typically uninteresting to the person or unrelated to the initial inquiry. Clearly, wonder could be helpful for education. It is pleasurable. It creates a hunger to know. It stimulates further interest and facilitates ease of learning. But these very qualities make the distortion of wonder a pleasurable vice. Wonder needs to be guided by studiousness.

Studiousness protects and preserves wonder from decaying into curiosity. Studiousness is a virtue classified under temperance: it orders our desire for knowledge. On the one hand, we are inclined to laziness and avoiding the effort of learning. One the other hand, we have a desire to know that can spiral out of control. Studiousness helps us avoid both extremes. Studiousness creates the framework to learn things that can only be appreciated with the passage of time. It helps us persevere in learning. Studiousness guides wonder by encouraging us to move beyond questions of what, when, where, and how, to questions of why, ultimately toward God.

Circling back to the point of this reflection, it helps to learn about the role of studiousness in human flourishing and achieving our final end in God. Appropriate deterrents to curiosity and rewards for studiousness are also helpful. But perhaps most helpful is a sensory-rich, emotionally powerful experience in which we witness someone suffering the disfigurement of curiosity or, even better, practicing studiousness in a beautiful way. Tell personal, sensory-rich, emotionally resonant stories of how studiousness helped you learn something worth learning. Share stories about curiosity run amok: Pandora's box, Digory ringing the bell in *The Magician's Nephew*, or Nathaniel Hawthorne's "Rappaccini's Daughter." These experiences involve the senses, evoke emotions, illuminate intellectual explanations, and motivate the will to practice studiousness. If we want to harmonize the senses and emotions with the intellect and will, we do not start with the intellect and will. We start with the senses and emotions and work our way to the intellect and will, harmonizing all to love God with heart, soul, mind, and strength.

Volume I: *Paideia to Monastic Education*

In a good education, wonder develops and matures as it inspires and is guided by the virtues of studiousness, docility, and integrity. Volume II reflects on docility. Volume III reflects on integrity. The next section of this volume explores pedagogy, activities, and resources for education, beginning with a practical guide for doing sensory-emotional formation, focusing on cultivating wonder.

PART TWO
The Workbook

CHAPTER I

Cultivating Wonder: A Practical Guide to Sensory-Emotional Formation

～ ～

SENSORY-EMOTIONAL FORMATION has four steps. The first step limits obstacles. The second step cultivates senses and emotions through direct contact with true, good, and beautiful experiences. The third step connects sensory-emotional formation to intellectual and spiritual formation by involving reflection and review. The last step develops a prudent plan for carrying out the other steps.

Applying this plan to wonder, we have the same steps. First, we remove obstacles to wonder. As noted in the reflection on sensory-emotional formation, this may mean addressing cultural expectations or trauma. In the case of wonder, we must make a special effort to address surfeit of stimulus, as well as two other obstacles: attachment to good grades and behaviors that fragment attention. Second, we cultivate wonder by offering experiences likely to inspire wonder and other emotions and in ways that directly engage the senses. Third, through reflection and review on those experiences, we help the intellect and will move closer to the true, good, and beautiful, that is, we build on sensory-emotional formation to do intellectual and spiritual formation.

Finally, we develop a plan for carrying out the other steps. The practices that cultivate wonder also cultivate the other emotions. To learn how to form wonder is to learn how to do sensory-emotional formation.

A. Remove Obstacles to the Cultivation of Senses and Emotions

(1) FOSTER DETACHMENT FROM GRADES

When students are worried about grades, they might not let themselves pursue learning unless it is demonstrably related to good grades. But many wonderful experiences, especially spiritual ones, lack a clear connection to academic or professional advancement. Therefore, offer ungraded assignments and opportunities for unspecified extra credit or, even better, for no reason, for fun. There should be no obligation to do the assignment, no possibility of failing or negative repercussions for not doing it. It should be fun for the teacher to review and offer an opportunity to connect with the student in shared wonder. It can be a great way to connect with parents in wonder. Tell them, "Look at this. This is something your child did for no reason, for fun. She didn't have to do this. Isn't this great?" Ideas for this kind of assignment include keeping a shelf of good books that are not part of official course reading, clever mathematics problems, creative writing assignments, illustrating course material, or student-designed projects related to and building on course material.

In a similar manner, give yourself interesting reading or other stimulus that offers no clear professional advantage. In

Volume I: *Paideia to Monastic Education*

The Accidental Creative, Todd Henry recommends that twenty-five percent of your stimuli be devoted to work, twenty-five percent devoted to personal or spiritual growth, and fifty percent devoted to things that fascinate you.

(2) AVOID BEHAVIORS THAT FRAGMENT ATTENTION

Avoid and encourage the avoidance of behaviors that fragment attention or overload the senses and emotions with conflicting experiences. For example, eat your lunch without using your phone or trying to work. Put away phones and screen-devices during in-person encounters. Avoid multi-tasking. A colleague described his renunciation of multi-tasking. Instead of trying to file papers and talk on the phone simultaneously or write emails during meetings, he did one thing at a time. If he was with a person or group, he gave his entire attention to them. To his surprise, not only was he able to give people more attention and better assistance, he also found that he completed his work faster.

(3) LIMIT "VISUAL NOISE"

Consider Josef Pieper's recommendation to fast from or set limits to stimuli. Examine how much news, social media, internet browsing, and other stimuli you consume. You may find it helpful to track this for a week or so to get a real idea about the kinds of stimuli you experience and the amount of time spent.

In a school, keep classrooms simple, beautiful, free of distraction, and easy to tidy and clean. To reduce the wasting of time and attention on fashion, status, and socio-economic comparisons, consider adopting student uniforms or a dress code, a faculty dress code, and a policy about the kinds of toys and gadgets students can bring to school.

Exercise prudence over the students' and your own personal consumption of national and local news, social media, and community "gossip." C. S. Lewis discouraged news consumption among adolescents:

> I think those are very wrong who say that schoolboys should be encouraged to read the newspapers. Nearly all that a boy reads there in his teens will be known before he is twenty to have been false in emphasis and interpretation, if not in fact as well, and most of it will have lost all importance. Most of what he remembers he will therefore have to unlearn; and he will probably have acquired an incurable taste for vulgarity and sensationalism and the fatal habit of fluttering from paragraph to paragraph to learn how an actress has been divorced in California, a train derailed in France, and quadruplets born in New Zealand.[1]

Aristotle observes that the young and immature are not ready to participate in discussions about politics because they lack experience and self-control. Until they have aged and matured, the study of current events and political issues wastes time and energy.[2]

---

1. C. S. Lewis, *Surprised by Joy* (New York: Harcourt, Brace, and Company, 1955), 159.
2. Aristotle, *Ethics*, I.3, 1094b29–1095a12.

Volume I: *Paideia to Monastic Education*

Even with years and maturity, the overconsumption of news and political discussion has its dangers. The negative impact of news consumption comes out in Timothy Tackett's work *The Glory and the Sorrow* about Adrien Colson (1727–1797), a Parisian lawyer who lived through the French Revolution. Colson was in his early sixties. He had celebrated the birth of the dauphin and expressed affection for the king and the Church throughout his entire life. According to Tackett, "the very concept of 'revolution' was altogether foreign to his thinking before the spring and summer of 1789."[3] Then his ideas altered dramatically.

What changed Colson? His correspondence contains no mentions of Voltaire, Rousseau, Diderot, or any other famous Enlightenment thinkers. Nor is there evidence that Colson owned or had read any of their works. Tackett identifies several influences, primarily the "flood" of print media. Colson's shift toward "more radical positions can be discerned" letter by letter in his new use of terms like "liberty," "equality," the "tyranny and despotism" of the previous regime, and "a return to the religion of the early church."[4] By 1794, Colson identified with the most revolutionary faction in Paris. In less than five years, media had helped to alter the trajectory of Colson's thought completely.

This gives food for thought about our own media consumption. We do not have unlimited time, attention, and energy. We are easily influenced. Limiting stimulus can safe-

---

3. Timothy Tackett, *The Glory and the Sorrow: A Parisian and His World in the Age of the French Revolution* (New York: Oxford University Press, 2021), 163.
4. Ibid., 165–166.

guard measured reflection and the maturation of thought at any age. Pieper writes that the man surfeited with visual noise "inevitably falls prey to the demagogical spells of any powers that be. 'Inevitably,' because such a person is utterly deprived even of the potential to keep a critical distance."[5] Studiousness limits obstacles to wonder.

B. *Offer Experiences That Inspire Wonder*

(1) CONTACT WITH GOD

Seek opportunities for yourself and your students to come in contact with God through the sacraments, Eucharistic Adoration, spiritual reading, prayer, and retreats. Show students the love of God through attention and compassion. Encourage friendships and forums for building good friendships.

(2) CONTACT WITH NATURE

Create opportunities for yourself and your students to come in contact with nature. A science course is a perfect forum for taking students outside, but anyone can take students outside to look at animal tracks, nesting birds, and changes in weather. Offer hikes, field trips, and stargazing.

(3) CONTACT WITH GREAT WORKS OF ART

Create opportunities for yourself and your students to experience great works of art: history, hagiography, music, art, film, literature, poetry, and fairy tales. If possible, try to

---

5. Pieper, "Learning How to See Again," 34.

experience things in the original, for example, the real church over a photograph, the whole work over an excerpt.

Works of art that praise wonder or discourage curiosity and a lack of wonder are helpful. For example, Ray Bradbury's *Fahrenheit 451* paints the picture of a grim future where people wile away the time in reckless driving or watching screens. Nobody asks questions. Growing frustrated, the main character counters: "We need to be really bothered once in a while. How long is it since you were *really* bothered? About something important, about something real?"[6]

Good stories engage the senses and inspire emotion. They help students recognize the true, good, and beautiful. They give a sense for right behavior and ordered emotion. Good characters experience compassion or want to be brave; they feel reverence in the presence of beauty. Weak characters succumb to jealousy or resentment; they cheat and betray their friends; they feel nothing in the presence of beautiful music. If you are a teacher, mentor, or leader, model the right response to truth in prayer, beauty in the liturgy or in nature, goodness in saints and fictional characters. Let students see your delight in the good and sorrow at the bad.

C. Reflect

Someone who begins to experience wonder can face a temptation. According to Fr. Clayton Thompson, this is the

---

6. Ray Bradbury, *Fahrenheit 451* (New York: Del Rey Books, 1978), 52.

temptation to "become a beauty junkie."[7] Instead of pondering and learning from a wonderful experience, one rushes on to the next experience. Intellectual and spiritual formation can encourage studiousness to restrain this impulse and gently direct a person to contemplate the wonderful experience. This section outlines some ways to engage in and foster reflection.

(1) ENGAGE WONDERFUL EXPERIENCES THROUGH ARTISTIC CREATION

Even more than "fasting" from visual noise, Pieper recommends engaging in artistic creation to revisit and engage more deeply with the sources of wonder. Drawing from life is especially helpful. I have taken students through drawing exercises from Betty Edwards' *Drawing on the Right Side of the Brain*. Then I have taken them to a church to pray and draw a subject of their own choosing: the tabernacle, the monstrance, or a station of the cross. I have taken them outside to sketch a leaf, a tree, or a scene. I have taken them to museums or shown great works of art and directed students to draw what they see. Any artistic activity that focuses attention on something for a long time is helpful, for example, writing a story or poem about something witnessed, copying a text in calligraphy, or writing an icon.

(2) REFLECT ON WONDERFUL EXPERIENCES

We can reflect in solitude or in communal discussion

---

7. Fr. Clayton Thompson, "Why Beauty Hurts," *Those Catholic Men*, November 2, 2016.

during or after a shared experienced. Seek opportunities to ask better questions, not only "what, when, where, and how" but also "why" questions. "Why" questions eventually lead back to God. Talk about experiences of wonder and share your own questions.

One of the best conversations my family ever had took place one Christmas when people began to discuss this question: Have you ever experienced a moment when you both wanted to cry and laugh? What was it and why do you think you felt that? The men of my family talked about being moved to tears by music and sunsets. We were talking about experiences that touch the soul on a deep level. I will always admire my former pastor because he was so open about discussing the marvels of the world. He would discuss going to county fairs and looking at winter tree branches and lilacs and reading poetry, all in the context of homilies and catechesis, asking huge questions: Why is this so beautiful? Why does this inspire a desire that is almost painful? What is this desire? What is it for? Where does it come from?

(3) CULTIVATE ATTENTION AND ATTEMPTS TO GROW IN UNDERSTANDING

Cultivate both the body's physical capacity for sustained attention and the virtue of studiousness. This undermines obstacles to learning like sloth, curiosity, and a tendency to avoid the difficult while increasing the taste for truth, goodness, and beauty. As Aquinas writes, "perseverance in the thought diminishes the incentive to sin…the more we think about spiritual goods, the more pleasing they become to us, and forthwith sloth dies away."[8] Aquinas notes three ways to cultivate attention: delight in knowing, the challenge of an arduous good, and the gaps and lacunas in the work of our predecessors.[9]

Foster delight in knowing by helping students understand when they are succeeding in their quest to deepen understanding. Seek ways to construct student work to help students achieve small "wins" along the path of learning. Praise students individually and as a group for asking questions, for not being satisfied with easy and facile answers. Give both written praise and public recognition. Take a class through an example of student work that demonstrates eagerness to inquire.

Play up the challenge of different aspects of learning. Fuel interest in learning by using competition, a tool the Jesuits found effective. Students can compete against a standard, against their previous records and achievements, or against each other, as individuals, in teams within a class, grade against grade (for example, juniors against seniors), or school against school. A school can adopt a "house" system, sorting into groups with a particular ethos or charisma, heroes, patrons, customs, and traditions.

Harness the power of mistakes and lacunae. When students discover possible flaws or lacunae in work, it can motivate them to study and seek ways to amend these flaws and

---

8. Thomas Aquinas, *Summa Theologiae*, II-II, q. 35, a. 1, ad 4.
9. Ibid., q. 33, a. 3, body; I-II, q. 37, a.1, body and ad 1; I-II, q. 40, a. 8, Body; Thomas Aquinas, *Commentary on the Metaphysics of Aristotle*, translated by John P. Rowan, vol. 1 (Chicago: Henry Regnery Company, 1961), V.2, L.1, §287.

fill the gaps. Certainly, we need to proceed with prudence. It is easy for the young and inexperienced to "spot" lacunae where there are none. It is easy stop learning from predecessors in the excitement of seeking lacunae. Thomas Aquinas, John Henry Newman, Karol Wojtyła, and Joseph Ratzinger saw that different aspects of theology could be developed and clarified. But they also submitted with docility to the Church in matters of faith. They built on their predecessors because they reverenced them. We should proceed with docility and prudence as these giants did and adapt the tool to the age and maturity of the students.

This can take many forms. For example, I had a friend who was using a Latin textbook with her daughter. They discovered the work had many grammatical and typographical errors. This turned into an unexpectedly fun exercise: take a red pen, identify the Latin errors, and correct them. When teaching nature observation, I sometimes crafted a deliberately terrible observation (hasty drawing, missing information, and a vague description full of self-referential adjectives like "gross.") Then I shared it with the class to see how it could be improved. A colleague plays "The Mistake Game" in which student teams deliberately introduce a mistake into their work. Other groups try to identify the mistake. This technique can work in many subjects: math, translation, grammar, physics, history, etc. In addition to cultivating reflection, this practice trains the ability to correct one's own and other's work and to accept that mistakes are part of learning. With older students, good paper topics and projects are born out of identifying an idea that has not been fully explored, argued, or presented.

(4) REVISIT WONDERFUL EXPERIENCES AND REJOICE IN NEW INSIGHTS

After some time has passed, revisit a wonderful experience. Teach or share the experience with another and learn from his fresh encounter. Review something from the perspective of time passed, new experiences, new knowledge, or new insight. Recognize and celebrate any ways in which understanding has developed.

The following practices assist with this kind of review. Try them or assign them to your students. Collect responses or include them in a portfolio and calendar to review them at some future date: the end of a book, unit, semester, course, year, or entire school career.

REREAD, REVISIT, REWRITE

Reread and discuss a book you have already read. Revisit a place you have already seen. Review something you have already studied: a concept, a picture, a science experiment. Rewrite an old paper. For example, a colleague asked students in their final semester to find and improve a paper written in their very first semester. The students were not only amazed by the enormous improvement in their writing, but many also took the opportunity to improve the argumentation and insights of the original papers.

JOURNALS

Keep a journal. This can take many forms: a nature journal, a *florilegium* of favorite quotations, or a prayer journal. Any written or visual record can work if it allows the author to revisit previous understanding and recognize change both in the world and in himself. Calendar to review this journal after the passage of time.

LETTER TO THE FUTURE

Write a letter to yourself in the future about an experience and the questions and insights it raised. Write your guesses at future outcomes and possible answers related to your experience and questions. Calendar to read this letter and compare the real future and its insights to the past.

DEFINITIONS

At the beginning of a book, unit, semester, course, or year, complete a writing prompt on a big question. For example, "What is science?" or "What is prayer?" or "What kind of book is this?" Calendar to revisit the original answer and compare it with how you would answer that question now.

WHAT DID YOU LEARN?

At the end of a unit, semester, course, or year, complete this writing prompt: *Write down everything you learned. What still puzzles you?* Calendar to reread the response at some future date.

PORTFOLIOS

Keep a portfolio of completed work. This can include all the work or your choice of the best work. The portfolio can include anything: essays or written reflections, completed math problems, drawings, maps, etc. Revisit the items in the portfolio and reflect on how the work and understanding have developed.

D. Make a Plan

The final step exercises studiousness to develop a plan that removes obstacles, affords wonderful experiences, and reflects. Make a plan to cultivate wonder in yourself and in anyone you mentor. Encourage others to do the same. Begin by reviewing your time and considering these questions.

- Inventory: What kinds of stimulus do I typically encounter? Besides that which is necessary for work, how much is devoted to learning, spiritual growth, or personal interest? Could I limit or eliminate something to make room for better stimuli or for time to reflect and review on the stimuli I have already experienced?
- How much time daily or weekly could I devote to direct contact with God through prayer, nature, and great works of art?
- How much time daily or weekly could I devote to engaging in artistic creation?
- How much space do I leave in my week to ponder what I am learning through school, work, leisure, and my interaction with other people?
- How much time do I leave in my course for wonder? For example, do I build in time for questions? Am I able to throw out my lesson plan to give time to a deeper question if one arises? Could I deliberately introduce moments of silence?
- How much time do I leave in my course for reflection and review? Avoid trying to cram too much material, homework, and activity into a class or

Volume I: *Paideia to Monastic Education*

course. Focus on key points, and like the Jesuits, build in time for review and mastery of material before moving on to new material.

CHAPTER 2

Physical Education, Song, Dance, and Manual Labor

From the Greeks to John Bosco, educators have recognized that physical activity is a critically important aspect of education. It honors and forms the human body. It facilitates sensory-emotional formation and paves the way for intellectual and spiritual formation. Provide students in all stages of development to engage regularly in such activities and in all forms of play, including free unstructured play, outdoor play, and forms of rough-and-tumble play. Reflect on ways to incorporate sports, games, physical exercise, song, dance, and manual labor in daily life.

A. *Physical Education*

Honor the body and model a love of the body, its capacities, and states: heartbeat, breathing, hunger, thirst, sleep, energy, stretching, calming, the ability to gesture, hold and manipulate tools, walk, run, crouch, leap, and dance. In addition to sports and games, incorporate other kinds of physical activity. Take a break and go out with the students to enjoy a windy day. Build in breaks of physical movement as part of class. Have students physically act out images in paintings and scenes in plays and novels. If you are calling students up to the board, for example, to diagram a sentence, translate, or write out a math problem, turn this into a game. Let individuals race to the board or group the students as teams and have them race in relays to complete work at the board. If your students are too antsy to attempt something that requires stillness and mental focus, have them work off excess energy with footraces or shooting a few baskets.

Build physical activity into the celebratory events of the school or parish. Offer hikes, stargazing, canoe trips, archery contests, bicycle tours, trips to the sea or the lake, or getting up to see the sunrise and eating a big celebratory breakfast afterward. Run a day of indoor games, outdoor sports, or all-school rounds of capture the flag.

I saw physical activity beautifully incorporated during a celebration for the Feast of Corpus Christi. The town of Orvieto, Italy, is famous for its Eucharistic procession and pageantry. What I remember best was the way Orvieto celebrated the vigil with youth footraces. The children of the town had been divided by neighborhood. Teams wore different colored t-shirts: yellow, blue, red, and green. The track ran around the cathedral. The sun had gone down and teenagers on Vespas raced around the cathedral lighting up the track. Parents talked and laughed, ate and drank behind a rope cordon. Suddenly, the race began. The kids sprinted off around the cathedral. The parents exploded into exuberant cheers. Round and round the cathedral, little kids raced. Vespas roared. And parents cheered until one neighborhood was crowned with victory. It was loud, fun, and exhilarating, all in the shadow of the beautiful church where a Eucharistic miracle helped launch a universal feast to celebrate the body and blood of Our Lord.

B. *Singing and Dancing*

Build singing into a course. Teach a related historical song as part of a history or literature unit or just as a fun activity, something true, good, and beautiful. Teach a related historical dance as part of a history or literature unit. Take a class or the whole school to concerts and choir events. Host a visiting choir at the school or parish. Open or close a regular gathering, such as a class or weekly youth group meeting, by teaching a new song or singing an old one. Create and use song books. Make and share song mixes of good choral songs: folksongs, ballads, madrigals, hymns, and any good music that the students might not encounter without your help. Regularly revisit old songs. Expand the repertoire. Encourage participants to memorize the verses of multiple good songs. Then the community can participate in spontaneous singing. I have seen groups strike up and rejoice in their ability to sing "Salve Regina," "O Come All Ye Faithful," "Auld Lang Syne," and "The Parting Glass." It is a wonderful thing.

Build song and dance into the celebratory events of the school or parish. In addition to sacred music within the liturgy, build in space to sing a song during a feast. Host a weekly bonfire song night, St. Patrick's Day Irish-style session, or a

Burn's Night with song and poetry. Host a dance for a celebration. Teach and try multiple kinds of beautiful dances: swing dancing, waltzes, contra dance, reels, and square dancing. Several of these dances minimize the wallflower experience because they change partners or do not require partners at all. They encourage learning how to work with a partner or a group. They offer opportunities to cultivate rhythm and physical coordination.

C. *Manual Labor*

Many families involve their children in helping around the house or with a family business. But this manual labor is not always considered part of education. Take a page from monastic education and make sure that young people are learning from manual labor. Physical work offers many opportunities to learn about the dignity of work and to cultivate body and soul.

If you are a parent, consider your child's opportunities to learn the meaning and dignity of good work. Opportunities can include handicraft hobbies, household chores, work-study at school, and for older children, working in a family business or part-time job.

Use work as an opportunity to teach about work in light of the cross. Tell your child about the work of St. Joseph, Jesus, and the apostles. Tell your child the story of Genesis and the Fall of man. Tell your child about your struggles with work. Make sure your child has an opportunity to talk about the difficult aspects of work. Let your child help you with work or work with him on his tasks. Occasionally, do your child's task in the way he is doing it and see if the task could be improved. Sometimes children do not realize a task could be improved. You can help them if you understand the task and its challenges. Work with your child to remedy unduly burdensome aspects of the work.

Use work as an opportunity to teach about work in light of God as maker of heaven and earth. Make sure your child has opportunities to work with and for others so he can develop a sense for the relational aspect of work. Make sure your child has opportunities to try a wide variety of tasks and to engage in some that help him develop his gifts and abilities. Grant your child increasing autonomy. Have him choose a task. Have him plan and execute the timing, tools, and steps of a task. Allow your child to make decisions, even mistakes. Help him to learn from those mistakes. Provide feedback and the opportunity to try again. Talk with your child regularly about what he is learning through his work. Praise your child when he does a good job, point out what is done well, praise him for persevering in work, and thank him for his contribution.

If you work in a school or parish setting, incorporate manual labor, and adapt the parent recommendations for discussion, collaboration, creativity, autonomy, feedback, and praise. Support the home and family as the first school of work. Make it easier for parents to engage in the formation described above. For example, allow what parents and children are doing at home to "count" as a project for school or club.

Provide further reflection on the dignity of work through

discussion or talks. For example, theology teachers can introduce Catholic social teaching. History teachers can connect work to units on monasticism or the rise of secular nineteenth and twentieth-century theories of work. Literature teachers can connect work to texts that explore themes of labor and industry, from *Charlotte's Web* to various books by Charles Dickens.

Work with students to care for an area of the school or parish grounds. Allow students to engage in handicrafts at appropriate times. For example, Mary Pat Donoghue relates how St. Jerome Academy students are free to work on knitting and similar activities during read-aloud time. Collaborate on a physical project, like serving a meal to the school or building an outdoor shrine. Create and tend a garden, raise an animal, or even participate in the life of a farm. In *Little Women*, each daughter designs and tends her own garden. A key element of the pedagogy at Saint Martin's Academy (Fort Scott, Kansas) is a farm with livestock and seasonal vegetables. Volume III relates modern renewal efforts working in the monastic tradition and the tradition of Jean Baptiste de la Salle to combine practical training with the liberal arts. If you lead a school or parish, consider ways to incorporate manual labor as part of an integrated Catholic education. Help home, school, and parish be true schools of work

CHAPTER III

Nature Study and Journaling

Previous chapters note the importance of reflection and contact with nature, God's first book. This chapter gives ideas for nature study and reflection through journaling. Aristotle, Aquinas, and numerous artists, scientists, philosophers, and theologians down to our own day understood that learning begins not with theory, not with hypothesis, but with close sensory attention to the things at hand. Only from this solid foundation, with the skills to notice, observe, and distinguish, can we move to further study.

Nature study is good preparation for studying both the *quadrivium* and STEM subjects in a manner informed by the *quadrivium*'s reverence for the created order. Nature study has much in common with the *trivium*. Like grammar, nature study teaches students to recognize and name things, parts of things, and groups of things. Like logic, nature study teaches students to discern difference, patterns, sequence, and cause and effect in the natural world. Like rhetoric, nature study teaches students to express what they observe and notice in increasingly accurate descriptions, diagrams, and sketches. Like the *trivium*, nature study prepares students to embark on the *quadrivium* and all mathematical and scientific studies with trained senses, powers of observation, reverence, and wonder.

A. *Goals*

- To observe well and set down observations in detailed, colored sketches and written descriptions that include logistical details like the date, time, and location, and increasingly accurate vocabulary.
- To learn more about the natural world, especially to recognize and name things and the parts of things at different stages of life or development.
- To experience what can be learned by gathering data over time, for example, to notice change.
- To become more interested in and attentive to the beauty of the natural world, not just "for homework."

B. *Possible Elements of a Single Observation*

- Date, time, and location.
- Note or picture indicating weather and estimated humidity, temperature, wind speed, and direction.
- One or more line drawings or colored sketches attentive to detail. Besides sketches, students can also include the tracing of objects, rubbings (bark, leaves, fossils), pressed flowers, or a smear of color from the juices of a plant or berry.
- A written description or series of comments that

use descriptive adjectives and note things like change, size, movement, number, color, shape, scent, and other sensory details.
- Identification and labeling (after the teacher has begun to introduce terminology).
- To facilitate feedback, have students number the pages of the journal. Sometimes journal pages are too beautiful to mark with comments and sometimes there is no room on the page. Give feedback on a separate sheet of paper or note system, referencing the page numbers.

C. *Process*

Nature journaling can be assigned at any age once a student is comfortable with writing and can sit still for ten minutes or more.

(1) OBSERVE

Give students regular time to look at objects from the natural world and make an observation in their nature journal. A good amount of time is twenty to thirty minutes, two to five times a week. Have each student choose a spot a little distance from other students and stand or sit down. Students work in silence, observing, sketching, and writing. During this time, move from student to student, giving help and encouragement as needed. If possible, take students outside. In good weather, students can head outside and find an object or area to observe. Or they can return to an object or area chosen earlier. If you want them to return to a specific place, have them note and draw landmarks on the first visit so they can easily find the place again.

(2) GIVE FEEDBACK

Collect journals after students have completed eight to twelve observations and give feedback. Indicate tendencies to omit key elements and ways to improve. For students who need a further challenge, see chapter seven of the Workbook for resources to improve and vary observations. Continue to gather nature journals and give feedback every two to three weeks.

(3) INTRODUCE TERMS

After three to six weeks of observation, begin to introduce names, terms, and vocabulary. Adjust the rate of this process and the number of terms to the age of your students. Have students begin to use them in their descriptions. Reinforce familiarity with two kinds of questions. Point it out, for example, a thorax, and ask: What do you call this? Or ask: Could someone find me an example of beaver activity or river deposition out here? Then discuss the validity of student suggestions.

(4) REVISIT, REFLECT, DISCUSS

As students learn new terms, read, or make new observations, encourage them to revisit earlier observations and add notes and commentary in light of new learning.

Near the end of each quarter or semester, hold an open-ended discussion in which students pool observations and discuss what they have noticed over time. Also consider holding an "art show" in which students display and view one another's best sketches from the semester.

D. *Ideas for Enriching the Process*

(1) IDEAS FOR FAIR WEATHER

Broaden your definition of fair weather. A lot of weather is "fair" if your students have good boots or wellingtons, hats, coats, gloves, and access to a mudroom, locker-room, or uncarpeted space to store and change gear. It is great to take people out on snowy, muddy, or misty days. Here are some other ideas for fair weather.

(*i*) *Have a Class or School Garden.* Take students to work in the garden, caring for and observing plants at various stages. Involve the students in planning the garden, tilling the soil, planting, tending, and winterizing it.

(*ii*) *Visit an Outdoor Classroom.* Build an outdoor classroom in an area sheltered by trees and frequented by animals. Set up benches or tree stumps for seats and install some birdfeeders nearby. Teach outside or take students out to do an observation. Consider involving students in building the classroom.

(*iii*) *Mapping.* Take students outdoors and walk around an area. In the next class, ask them to draw an overhead map of the area they explored. Compare student maps with a real map or take them back outside to compare and amend their maps with the real terrain. Show interesting maps like J. R. R. Tolkien's maps of Middle-Earth to give students ideas for making more maps.

(*iv*) *Silhouette Comparisons.* While trees are still green, have students draw the silhouette of a deciduous tree or tree line and color in their guess for the hues that will appear when the trees change colors and prepare to drop their leaves. Later, when the trees do change colors, have students draw the silhouette of the same deciduous tree or tree line and color in the actual hues. Compare the two observations.

(*v*) *Give Prompts Based on John Muir Laws' Suggestions.* Ask students to examine the parts of an object, then back up and look at the whole object. Ask them to draw an image of themselves next to the object for comparison or add another kind of size reference. Suggest they draw a scale or make a note to indicate if the drawing is shrunk or enlarged and by about how much.

Ask students to complete the following writing prompts drawn in part from Kerry Ruef's Private Eye Project: "I notice… I wonder… It reminds me of… I see… I hear… It smells like… It feels…"

Ask students to keep a list or collection of kinds of observations. Laws suggests lists ideas like seed pods, berries, and winter twigs. When students go out to observe, suggest they do an observation that adds to one of their lists.

Give each student a long piece of string. Ask students to use the string to form a circle on the ground. Have them sit in the circle, observing and recording everything in the circle.

Have students choose two subjects that appear to be members of the same or similar species. Ask students to compare them.

Ask students to storyboard an event or draw a series of events in square images like a graphic novel. Laws used this method to depict an observation of watching a crow wash a worm before eating it!

(*vi*) *Sound Page.* Use the template on the next page. Read through the template with students and explain the process. Then go outside or wherever observations are taking place. In this exercise, the student listens and records where sounds are coming from in relation to him. He also describes them, using pictures or written notes or descriptions. Students should try to be silent, noting even quiet, ongoing noises. Once students are familiar with the exercise, you can dispense with the template. Students can simply draw a circle and mark a dot in their nature journal, recording time, date, weather, and other notes.

SOUND PAGE TEMPLATE

Name: _____

Date: _____

E   YOU   W

MARK THE POSITION OF THE SUN

Time: _____ AM / PM to _____ AM / PM

1. Describe or draw a little picture to indicate the weather:

2. Describe the quality of the air, for example, crisp, humid, dry, cold, foggy, etc.

3. Temperature feels like _____. Actual Temperature is _____. How close were you?

4. Is there wind today? Draw an arrow on the circle on the next page to show which way the wind is blowing.

5. Estimate which way you are facing: north, south, east, west? Draw an arrow on the circle on the next page to indicate the direction you are facing.

6. Listen.

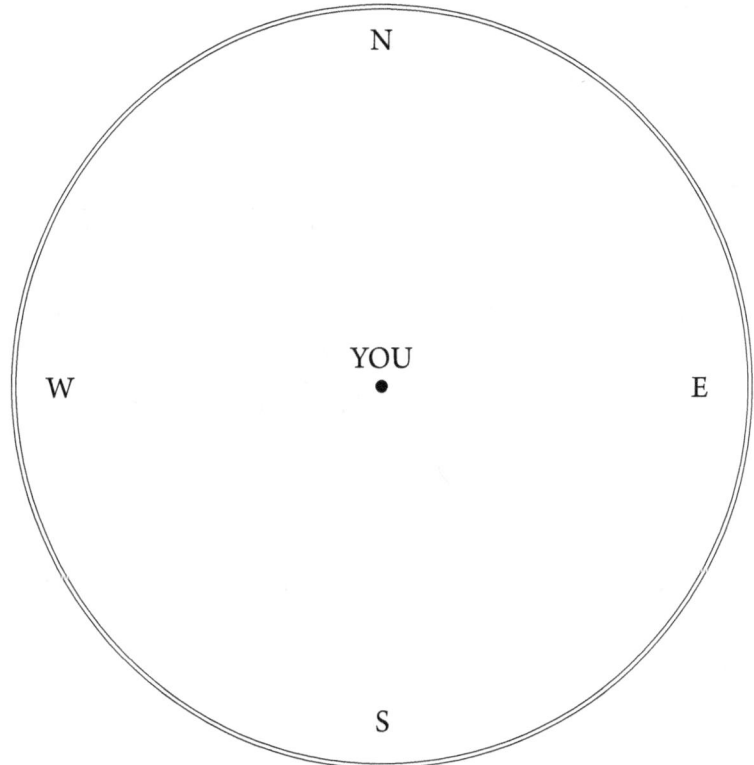

Each time you hear a sound, mark its position in the circle relative to you. Here are some ways to represent the sound:
- A little sketch (a stream, a squirrel, a dog);
- A word to indicate a sound ("wooooossssh" for wind, "crack!" for a snapping twig, "Arf! Arf!" for a barking dog);
- A phrase or sentence to describe the sound (like "low humming" or "repeated whistling noise far away").
- Try to describe the sounds: their volume ("soft, medium, loud"), their pitch (high, low), intensity (loud, soft), their number and duration (five times, ongoing, a few seconds), and proximity (nearby, next to me, behind the house).

SAMPLE SOUND PAGE

Name: GWEN ADAMS

Date: 1/23/25

E • YOU • W

MARK THE POSITION OF THE SUN

Time: 2 AM / (PM) to 2:15 AM / (PM)

1. Describe or draw a little picture to indicate the weather:

SUNNY, BRIGHT BLUE SKY. ONE CLOUD SHAPED LIKE THIS △ MOVING EAST.

2. Describe the quality of the air, for example, crisp, humid, dry, cold, foggy, etc.

COLD AND DRY.

3. Temperature feels like __25°__. Actual Temperature is __30°__. How close were you? 5 DEGREES!

4. Is there wind today? Draw an arrow on the circle on the next page to show which way the wind is blowing. YES!

5. Estimate which way you are facing: north, south, east, (west)? Draw an arrow on the circle on the next page to indicate the direction you are facing.

6. Listen.

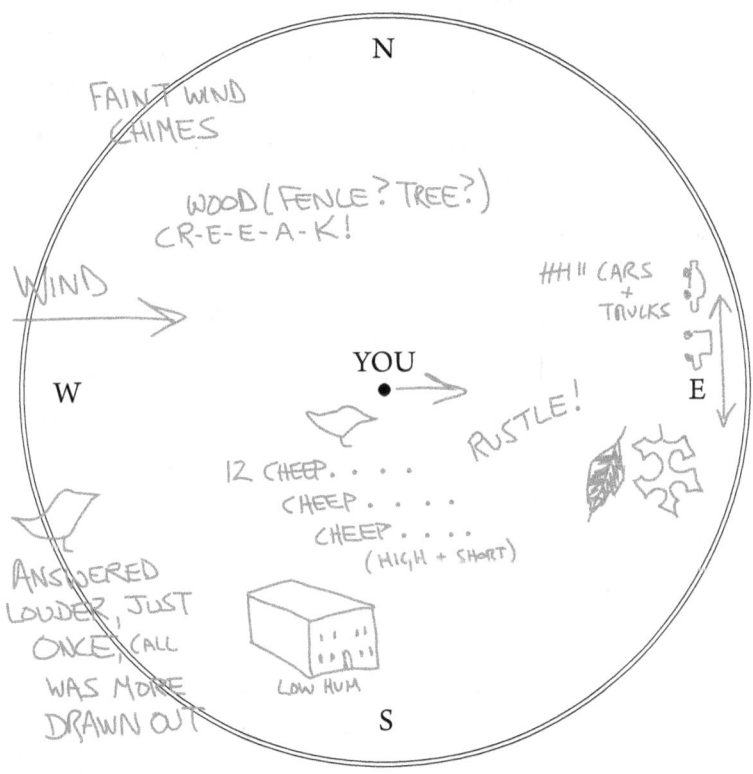

Each time you hear a sound, mark its position in the circle relative to you. Here are some ways to represent the sound:

- A little sketch (a stream, a squirrel, a dog);
- A word to indicate a sound ("wooooossssh" for wind, "crack!" for a snapping twig, "Arf! Arf!" for a barking dog);
- A phrase or sentence to describe the sound (like "low humming" or "repeated whistling noise far away").
- Try to describe the sounds: their volume ("soft, medium, loud"), their pitch (high, low), intensity (loud, soft), their number and duration (five times, ongoing, a few seconds), and proximity (nearby, next to me, behind the house).

(2) IDEAS FOR INCLEMENT WEATHER

(i) *Improve Drawing Skills.* Improve drawing skills with exercises from Betty Edward's *Drawing on the Right Side of the Brain* and *Drawing on the Artist Within*. Many students hold back in nature study because they are uncomfortable with the quality of their drawings. Edward's exercises tend to produce rapid improvement and give students confidence for further drawing. Try some of the following exercises.

- Upside-down drawing: Start with Edward's examples—Pablo Picasso's *Portrait of Igor Stravinsky* and the line drawing of the German horse and rider. Also try portions of the line sketches in *Audubon's Birds of America Coloring Book*, for example, a single bird.
- Drawing negative space: Start with Edward's recommendation of a chair or subject with clean straight lines and geometric "negative spaces." Another subject is a group of pencils or pens in a clear glass. After students are beginning to get used to this exercise, try them with organic subjects. A spray of twigs or leafy branch in a vase yields a beautiful negative space drawing.
- Drawing an object with variations in shading. Edwards starts students with a monochrome black and white drawing before repeating this exercise with an image that also varies in color. I often suggest students try this exercise upside down on their first try.
- A gesture exercise: This timed exercise shows fifteen images in rapid succession. Students sketch

what they see within the space of a minute before shifting to the next image and sketching. The exercise teaches students to perceive and draw edges quickly. Because animals move and the wind stirs plants, these can be daunting subjects for sketching in the field. This exercise frees students to choose such complex subjects for nature study.

(*ii*) *Indoor Observations.* Keep a collection of things indoors and offer them as subjects for drawing. Such items could include nests, feathers, blown eggs, shells, rocks, piles of different soil, bark, cross sections of wood, dried plants, living potted plants, cut flowers, seeds, nuts, or bones. If you have school pets, a fish-tank, or winter birds visiting your outdoor feeder, offer these for observation. Try the gesture exercise to get students used to drawing quickly.

- Assign students or student groups to choose two objects and compare them.
- Have students choose an object and look at it carefully without writing or sketching. Then remove the object from view and let the student complete an observation from memory. Bring out the object again and let the student compare, contrast, and amend the observation.
- Play bird calls for the students. Have the students describe what they hear. You can have them skip the sketch or have them try to capture visually what they hear.
- Do an indoor sound page. It is preferable to take the students to a larger relatively quiet space, like

an empty gym, chapel, cafeteria, or library, but this can also be done in a classroom.

(*iii*) *Games.*
- Play an occasional observation game. Have the students work as a team to look around the room. Send them out and change two or three things. Bring the students back in and see if they can guess what changed.
- Play SET, a mathematical game in which players attempt to notice and recognize patterns of similarity and difference.

E. *Helping Students to Improve Their Observations*

If students are struggling with sketching and coloring, give them an occasional break. Have them list the colors they see. Have them draw a grid of colors that appear in the object, using arrows to indicate areas where various colors appear on the object. Or take some time to work through the drawing exercises of Betty Edwards.

Create and present a deliberately poor observation and have students suggest ways to improve it.

If some students tend toward brief and hasty descriptions or tiny sketches, require them to work for a set period or to fill a certain area of space in their journal with sketches or diagrams.

Also try the following exercise. Pair or group students. Have them complete an individual observation of the same subject. Each will notice something that the other misses. Each will do something that would improve the other's observation. Then ask them to review and discuss one another's observations, getting new perspective and insights about how to improve their own observations.

Early on, after you have had a chance to review student nature journals, hold a Socratic Discussion to improve descriptions.

F. *Socratic Discussion about Descriptive Terms*

Sometimes students need help to improve the quality of their descriptions. Some descriptors tell more about a student's subjective experience than about the object observed, for example, adjectives like cool, lame, pretty, weird, or gross. Better descriptors evoke the five senses, for example, bristled, green, sour, wide as a penny, or sharp. Begin the discussion in this way:

Ask: *What are the five senses?*

Then draw the following chart on the board.

SIGHT:

SOUND:

TOUCH:

SMELL:

TASTE:

Ask: *What kinds of things can our senses tell us about something?*

Write student answers on the board under the appropriate categories. Solicit answers that cover the wide variety of things that senses apprehend: shapes, sizes, colors, hues, movement, how light reflects off something (matte or glossy); sounds, volume, pitch, rhythm; tastes; smells; tactile sensations, texture, temperature, movement.

Select a vague descriptor that comes up regularly in student nature journals, for example, "cool" or "gross." Write the word on the board and solicit ideas from the students about what the descriptor communicates. Write suggestions on the board. Continue to solicit ideas from the students until you have descriptors with clearly different meanings. For example, students might suggest that "cool" means "dangerous" while others suggest that it means "shiny."

Older students will quickly grasp that vague descriptors can be improved with more specific ones. Solicit ways to improve vague descriptors with specific ones evoking the five senses.

If students are younger and need a little more help to understand the weakness of vague descriptors, point out the alternate definitions of a vague descriptor like "cool" and ask, "Do these alternate definitions mean the same thing?" Then try a game. Think of an object without telling the students what it is. Choose a weak descriptor, for example, anthropomorphized descriptions (sad, lonely, thoughtful), hyperbole ("ridiculously loud"), or general facts ("these are in danger of extinction.") Write the descriptor on the board. Give students a few chances to guess the object associated with this description. Students will probably fail because weak descriptors do not describe well. Reveal the answer and solicit better ways to describe the object.

If helpful, try another game to solidify the point. Think of an object without telling the students what it is. It should be something which can be described with some of the recent student suggestions for strong descriptors. You can also add a few additional strong descriptors to the board. Tell the students, "I'm thinking of an object that could be described with some of these words." Circle the applicable descriptors and see if the students can guess what you are thinking. This time, at least some of the students might be able to guess the object because the descriptors are more specific and rich in sensory detail.

This concludes the chapter on nature study. One beauty of the practice is that anyone can incorporate it into their coursework, not just science teachers. It is a great help for anyone teaching a piece of literature with direct references to plants, trees, or other parts of nature. Any age can benefit from the practice. Although the practice improves with regularity, one can benefit even from rare, occasional practice.

CHAPTER IV

Reading Aloud

〜 〜

READ ALOUD in class and involve students in reading aloud. With older students and faculty, also try reading plays aloud together. One of the reasons Rebecca Bellingham advocates reading aloud is because it provides students with a real-time model for learning. Students can see a teacher stumble over an unfamiliar word, ask questions, try to remember earlier important information, or experience wonder and surprise. Thought is normally a silent, internal process, but reading aloud can incarnate it, rendering it visible for students who are learning how to learn. Bellingham also relates a story about crying while she read the end of *Charlotte's Web*. When a teacher expresses delight or pain, he models to the students what is good and bad, what is worthy of delight and what should evoke sympathy or righteous anger. Thus, reading aloud is a powerful tool for sensory-emotional formation.

Some texts lend themselves to good read-aloud experiences with K–12 students. That is, they are excellent stories with varied characters, good dialogue, rich vocabulary, and beautiful sentence construction. Many of these works can be found in audiobook form with excellent narrators. Listening to good readers via audiobook helps pronunciation and gives examples for improving diction, rhythm, timbre, and volume. See chapter seven of the Workbook for a list of good read-aloud authors and audiobook readers. The recommendations for reading aloud are based in part on ideas from Bellingham's *The Artful Read-Aloud: 10 Principles to Inspire, Engage, and Transform Learning*, Lyle Vernon Mayer's *Fundamentals of Voice and Articulation*, the practice of the Cana Academy literature guides, and other resources listed in chapter seven of the Workbook.

A. *Goals*

- To model the process of learning to students.
- To model delight in that which should delight and pain in that which should cause pain.
- To learn from great stories in a communal experience that involves the whole person.
- To cultivate student senses, especially listening, imagination, and memory, as well as the emotions, understanding, literacy, and the ability to express and develop understanding through discussion and writing.

B. *Preparation*

If you have read the book before or know it well and have done a few read-alouds, reading aloud can be done without preparation. Just jump in and practice! Otherwise, complete these steps.

(1) DETERMINE HOW MUCH TIME YOU WILL NEED

Bellingham recommends that K–8 students experience reading aloud for one to two-and-a-half hours a week, preferably a little every day. Lester Laminack regularly reads aloud to his college and graduate students. Estimate how long it would take to read the entire book aloud. Time yourself reading a section or get an estimate from an existing audiobook version. Then estimate how long it would take to discuss the entire book. Use this chart to estimate time.

TYPE OF WORK (narrative work, such as fiction, history, biography, saint or scripture story)	ONE PAGE (narrative work in 4"–6" x 6"–9" or picture-book in 9" x 11")	DISCUSSION RATE PER PAGE
GRADE 7+	1 page	2.5–5 minutes
GRADE K–6	1 page	1–2.5 minutes
PICTURE-BOOKS with 1–2 paragraphs of text	1 page	0.5–1 minute
PICTURE-BOOKS with less text	1 page	0.5 minutes

(2) MAKE A SCHEDULE

Make a rough schedule, first for the whole book, and then for the first class with reading aloud. Add your estimates and compare to the time available. Portion text and time accordingly: pages to read aloud, pages to assign for homework, and the number, length, and focus of discussions. Determine times to pause and ask questions or initiate reflection. Note what to eliminate if you are running out of time.

C. *Process*

(1) READ ALOUD

With a picture book or small group, sit down and have students draw near you. With a chapter book or group larger than eight to ten students, stand to read. Relax your facial muscles and body. Take a deep, sweet breath. Stand tall with good posture. Make eye contact with students and smile. Begin!

Use your voice, facial expressions, and gestures to help tell the story. Continue to make eye contact. Bellingham describes a time when she planned a discussion only to realize her students were enthralled and wanted to keep reading and another time when she planned to read to the end of a section, only to realize that her students needed a chance to move their bodies and talk. Read the room and adjust your plan as necessary. Model real-time learning and let students see your interior experience.

(2) Pause to Develop Imagination, Memory, Emotions, and Understanding

Pause to develop imagination, memory, emotions, and understanding. The following discussion and reflection formats can be adapted into follow-up written reflections.

(i) Pause for Three Kinds of Discussion
- Interior discussion: Ask students to ponder silently in their own minds about some aspect of the reading. Or ask them to write for a short time about some aspect of the reading.
- Discussion with a partner: Ask students to discuss some aspect of the reading with one or two students nearby.
- Whole group discussion: Pose a question and discuss as a group.

(ii) Pause for Three Kinds of Reflection
- Pause 1: Have students use their own words to summarize the story. If they have finished the book, they can summarize the whole story. Otherwise, they can summarize the story up to the point where you paused for reflection.
- Pause 2: Ask students to imagine dialogue or inner monologues. Students can use their imaginations and clues in the text to guess at the inner lives of characters. Students can silently imagine dialogue or inner monologues, or they can vocalize and share them with fellow students. This gives a sense

for the quality and nature of a student's imagination, memory, and understanding.
- Pause 3: Pose and discuss good questions. Try adapting questions from the following list to suit the work in question.

(3) GOOD QUESTIONS FOR NARRATIVE WORKS

Tailor questions around specific sensory details in the text: persons, places, things, shapes, sizes, colors, hues, movement, how light reflects off something (matte or glossy); sounds, volume, pitch, rhythm; tastes; smells; tactile sensations, texture, temperature, movement.

(i) At the Beginning of a Book
- What are you noticing about this character, relationship, or place?
- How would you describe him, her, it, or them?
- How are these people or things connected? Work together to draw a family or relationship tree.
- What else are you noticing?
- What ideas or questions are you starting to have about this character, relationship, place, or time?
- Take a moment: Can you see the character or scene in your mind? Pretend you are in that scene. What do you see? Hear? Smell? Taste? Feel? If you reached out and touched this character or this object in the reading, what would it feel like?

(ii) In the Middle of a Book
- Take a moment: What have we learned about this

character, relationship, or place? Now what are you noticing about this character, relationship, or place?

- Does it or do they seem to be changing? How so?
- Does the old family or relationship tree need to be revised? Draw an updated family or relationship tree.
- What does this word mean in this context? What does this character mean when he says this? Does the story give us any clues? Does the character's conversation suggest anything? Does his behavior or manner suggest anything?
- What does this character believe about God, people, or reality? How did the character come to have these beliefs? Does the story give us any clues? Does the character's conversation suggest anything? Does his behavior or manner suggest anything?
- Why is this character behaving in this manner? Why is he taking or failing to take this action? Does the story give us any clues? Does the character's conversation suggest anything? Does his behavior or manner suggest anything?
- Compare two characters. How does *this* character perceive, assess, or feel about this other character, event, or situation? What about the second character? Are there any similarities or differences in their perceptions, judgments, or feelings?
- Think about this repeated word or phrase, this object, or this thing that a character does. If it was different or omitted, what would change?

- Think about what just happened. How does this fit with what you already know? Does it change anything?
- What do you think is going to happen? How will this story end? What will the key characters do? (Sometimes, due to film adaptations of books, many students know the ending of a book. You can ask them to try to keep that information to themselves and to base their discussion contributions solely on what has been read so far.)

(iii) At the End of a Book
- Looking back, did any of the characters seem to change? How so?
- What do you think about the way this story ended?
- What ideas or questions do you have about this character, relationship, place, story, or idea we discussed?

D. *Ideas for Enriching the Process and Helping Students to Improve Their Reading Aloud*

(i) Take a Turn Reading Aloud. Assign students to take a turn reading aloud, one-on-one to a teacher, parent, or friend, or to the whole class. Help students grow in their ability to read aloud by recommending well-read audiobooks to students and their families.

(ii) Choral Exercises. Students engaged in choral singing learn many techniques helpful for reading aloud. They

stretch. They learn better breathing patterns. They improve resonance and tone by standing tall, lifting their eyebrows, and opening their mouths fully. They sing scales which extend the voice's range. They practice enunciating capacious vowels and clear consonants. Try these choral techniques or Cicely Berry's warm-ups from *The Actor and His Text*.

(*iii*) *Passing the Text*. Additionally, try exercises which help students take the text into their bodies. These are drawn from *The Actor and His Text*. Print and distribute a passage which fits on a single page. Berry uses Shakespeare. I have used passages from Ecclesiastes, Song of Songs, and *Beowulf*. Have students stand in a circle. Each student speaks a part of the text, stopping at a punctuation mark and "passing the text" to the student on his right. That is, at the punctuation mark, the next student begins speaking the text where the former left off. Some students may only have one word. From person to person, punctuation mark to punctuation mark, the text goes round the circle.

Try the exercise again, but now have each student shout his line boldly and with speed. You can start with the student who first began reading. Or start with whoever stands to the right of the last person to speak in the previous exercise.

Try the exercise again, but now have each student shout his line boldly and with speed, while making a gesture.

Change things up. There are no recommendations for volume or speed. Instead, have the students read the passage in unison. At each punctuation mark, students should move a different direction. If the room is small, students vary direction and movements within the limited space: standing tall, crouching low, a few steps to the right, a lunge forward. If the room is large, students can also add walking or running, still changing direction with each punctuation mark.

Return to the original exercise. Regroup into a circle and pass the text as before, but now have each student whisper his line. Make sure every syllable can be heard.[1]

At the end, ask: *What do you notice?*

These exercises cultivate active listening in addition to improved reading. Once students are comfortable "passing the text," try a work with dialogue and multiple characters. Have one student read the narrator's part while others read different characters, reading as a group in a Reader's Theater style.

(iv) *Try It Wrong.* Sometimes it helps a student break out of poor reading patterns if you suggest he exaggerate poor reading. Try a practice inspired by Judith Weston. Say, "Try it three ways. Do it wrong." Give examples. Here are some "wrong ways" to suggest.

- Resonance: Too breathy, hoarse, nasally, glottal, raspy, metallic, etc.
- Rate: Too fast, too slow, too many pauses, too few, no sense of rhythm, overly forced rhythm, etc.
- Pitch and Inflection: Too low, too high, monotone, too much random shifting in pitch, ending every sentence with a rising inflection like it is a question, ending every sentence with a downward inflection, etc.
- Volume: Too loud, too quiet, too little variety, too much variety, etc.

---

1. Cicely Berry, *The Actor and His Text* (New York: Scribner, 1988), 149–151.

- Diction: Mumbled or slurred, clipped, mispronounced, artificially over-pronounced, etc.

Let the student experiment with wrong ways. Use these attempts to identify something which works well. Then continue reading aloud.

(v) *Key Words Exercise.* This exercise is drawn from *A Shakespearean Actor Prepares* by Adrian Brine and Michael York. Give a student a slip of paper with a noun, for example, bowl or wheel. Ask the student to remember or imagine this word and its setting. Ask the student to picture all the sensory details of the word and the setting. Then, while picturing the word and its setting, have the student say the word aloud three times to a partner. Ask the partner to describe what came into his mind as the word was said. If others are present, ask them to share what they pictured.

Sometimes participants picture sensory details like those pictured by the student. Alternately, participants picture an object with similar states of being and emotional overtones. For example, I gave the word "wheel" to a student. While the participants pictured diverse sensory details, many shared a mental picture of a wheel with problems: a punctured white bicycle tire, a huge rusty wheel, a flat tire, a lone wagon wheel. In fact, the student had pictured a tire which burst and caused a terrible accident.

This exercise increases the power of words to communicate emotional resonance and rich sensory detail to the listeners. Now try the exercise with words in an assigned text. Have students to use the exercise to enrich key nouns in a passage to be read aloud.

(*vi*) *Portray the Story.* Let the students use their imaginations to portray events in a text.

Students can imagine an inner monologue or dialogue that did not appear in the text but could have, one that would make sense based on what is known so far about the story or reading. Have students write this inner monologue or dialogue.

Have students illustrate or draw timelines and maps related to characters and scenes in the text.

Invite younger students to use facial expression and gesture to embody parts of a story. Bellingham even invites students to make sound effects, for example, to growl with animal characters while she is reading. Have students create tableaus without movement, like a photograph or freeze-frame of a moment in the story. Have students dramatize a scene like Reader's Theater or an audio drama. Or have students stage the scene with physical movement, simple props, and costumes.

CHAPTER V

Leading a Socratic Discussion: A Variation on Didactic Instruction

Volume II outlines how to craft a great lecture and how to lead a discussion on poetry. Volume III outlines how to lead a text-based seminar and how to lead a discussion on art. This chapter outlines a pedagogy suited to subjects where lecture and didactic instruction are typically employed. It instructs through question-based discussion. For example, instead of giving a presentation on pine trees, or the Eucharist, or the end of Napoleon's empire, the teacher leads a discussion that answers questions like: "What are the distinctive characteristics of white pine versus pitch pine?" or "What does the Church teach about the Eucharist?" or "How did Napoleon finally lose power?"

This pedagogy guides participants to clear information. A lecture could do this faster, but questions are used for three reasons. First, to vary pedagogical method as a change of pace. Second, so that the students make the questions their own and thus develop a stake in discovering the answer. Third, to cultivate attention and powers of noticing in collaboration with others. You can tell a student that a white pine has needles in bundles of five. Or you can ask a student,

"How many needles are in this bundle?" Sometimes where direct instruction fails, a question can inspire eagerness to inquire. The purpose of the questions is not to assess learning but to instruct while awakening wonder. Therefore, I do not recommend grading this kind of discussion, although I do note if a student has demonstrated effort or recall of earlier course information.

A. *Goals*

- To instruct students about a topic.
- To awaken wonder and eagerness to inquire, giving students a personal stake in learning.
- To cultivate attention and powers of noticing in collaboration with others.

B. *Preparation*

(1) DESIGN THE DISCUSSION

(*i*) *Determine How Much Time You Will Need.* Plan for a discussion that lasts about two to three minutes times the age of the participants, with three to five minutes to introduce the discussion and five to ten minutes to summarize and close the discussion. Use this chart to estimate time. For adult students aged twenty-five and older, use twenty-five as the age.

Volume I: *Paideia to Monastic Education*

Discussion Step	Age of Participants	Minutes	Total Minutes
Introduction		3–5	3–5
Discuss Personal Stake Questions	___[AGE]___	× 1–1.5	=
Discuss Background Questions & Original Question	___[AGE]___	× 1–1.5	=
Ending		5–10	5–10
Total Time			=

For example, if my students are twelve years old, I need twelve to eighteen minutes for the Personal Stake Questions, and another twelve to eighteen minutes for the Background Questions, plus time to introduce and close the discussion.

(ii) Determine How Many Questions You Will Need. Use this chart to estimate the number of questions.

Number of Questions	Age of Participants		Total Questions
Personal Stake Questions	___[AGE]___	× 25%–75%	=
Background Questions & Original Question	___[AGE]___	× 25%–75%	=
Total Number of Questions			=

For example, if my students are twelve years old, I will need three to nine Personal Stake Questions and three to nine Background Questions.

(*iii*) *Choose a Topic.* Choose a topic that fascinates you and that you thoroughly understand. Thoroughly understanding a topic enables you to improvise questions during discussion if prepared questions are not working.

Turn some aspect of the topic into a "primary question." The question should be one that can be answered through discussion by a student or group of students working together and drawing on their own creativity, observation, and memory of material covered earlier in the course.

For example, topic: *The Battle of Marathon.*

Primary Question: *How did the Greeks defeat the Persians at the Battle of Marathon?*

(*iv*) *Brainstorm What Students Need to Know to Answer the Primary Question.*

Here is a sample brainstorm: *What do the students need to know at minimum to answer, "How did the Greeks defeat the Persians at the Battle of Marathon?"*

If I assign the reading on the Battle of Marathon, they can answer this question in a minute or two. If I hold this discussion right before I assign the reading, they could guess the correct answer. But they would have to have heard of other battles where outnumbered armies won through military strategy. Or to have played or seen games or sports with outflanking maneuvers. They would need to remember that Greece is a younger nation. They would need to remember the era: for example, no modern weapons, etc. Some knowledge of the geography would help.

(v) *Brainstorm What Students Need to Care About to Answer the Primary Question.*

Here is a sample brainstorm: *What do the students need to care about to answer, "How did the Greeks defeat the Persians at the Battle of Marathon?"*

It would help to identify as Athenians. They would need to remember that Persia was the dominant power at the time. If they admire Persia or figures like Cyrus the Great, their loyalties might be with Persia. That would complicate the discussion in a good way. We could discuss how to admire a country or person but also recognize failings or weaknesses. How to admire but not idealize or idolize. Students would need some awareness that the ancient world did not have our modern network of powerful alliances. The Greeks cannot call on a more powerful ally. Fleeing Greece to take refuge in another country will not guarantee safety. They would not be welcomed. It might not even be possible. The students would need to value courage and sacrifice. It would help if they valued the defense of one's native land, even at the cost of one's life.

(vi) *Turn the Brainstorm into a Series of Sub-Questions.* Turn the brainstorm into a series of sub-questions: Personal Stake Questions and Background Questions that can be answered with prior knowledge and creativity. Aim for a total number of sub-questions suited to the age of your group. Make sure you can answer the sub-questions with little to no reference to written notes.

Here are sample sub-questions to answer the Primary Question: "How did the Greeks defeat the Persians at the Battle of Marathon?" In this example, my students are twelve years old, so I am aiming for three to nine Personal Stake Questions and three to nine Background Questions. This is the original order, as they came to me.

PERSONAL STAKE QUESTIONS
- *Who has the most powerful empire at this time? What do we know about their power?*
- *What have they achieved in the past?*
- *Why does Persia want to invade?*
- *Is she justified? Why or why not?*
- *Does anyone here think we would be better off under Persian rule? Why or why not?*
- *Should we defend ourselves: What are the alternatives?*
- *Is Greece powerful? How does she compare to Persia?*
- *Should we defend ourselves? Why or why not?*
- *Would you, personally, take a part in the defense? Even if it cost you? Why?*

BACKGROUND QUESTIONS that can be answered with prior knowledge and creativity
- *If we defend ourselves, how would we do it? What is possible?*
- *If we defend ourselves, how would we do it? What is impossible?*
- *Is there some military maneuver or tactic that might work, even if we are fewer in number?*

Volume I: *Paideia to Monastic Education*

- Primary Question: *So how did the Greeks defeat the Persians at the Battle of Marathon?*

Order the sub-questions. Generally, a good order is to start with the questions that will inspire students to have a personal stake in answering the question. Continue with background questions that motivate students to remember what they already know, share ideas, and collaborate to reach the answer to the primary question.

Here are the sample sub-questions again, but now I have revised and reorganized them to ask in an optimal order.

PERSONAL STAKE QUESTIONS
(1) *Who has the most powerful empire at this time? What do we know about their power?*
(2) *What have they achieved in the past?*
(3) *Is Greece powerful? How does she compare to Persia?*
(4) *Why does Persia want to invade?*
(5) *Is she justified? Why or why not?*
(6) *Does anyone here think we would be better off under Persian rule? Why or why not?*
(7) *Should we defend ourselves? Why or why not? What are the alternatives?*
(8) *Would you, personally, take a part in the defense? Even if it cost you? Why?*

BACKGROUND QUESTIONS that can be answered with prior knowledge and creativity
(1) *If we defend ourselves, how would we do it? What is impossible?*

(2) *If we defend ourselves, how would we do it? What is possible?*

(3) *Is there some military maneuver or tactic that might work, even if we are fewer in number?*

(4) Primary Question: *So how did the Greeks defeat the Persians at the Battle of Marathon?*

(vii) *Draft an Opening Script.* Draft notes or a short opening script for beginning the discussion and setting the scene. The script should review important background information. It could suggest a narrative or scenario about the topic and have the group identify with characters in that narrative or scenario.

Here is a sample script for opening a discussion on the Battle of Marathon.

> TEACHER: (Adopting a booming voice and physical stance, as if making a speech at a political assembly or war-room)
>
> So. The year is about 490. We are the city of Athens. I don't need to tell you what's going on. You know it as well as I do. It's hard to believe almost ten years have passed since the Ionian Revolt first began. We sent military support. Emperor Darius crushed the revolt, but he didn't stop there. He believes the best defense of Persian territories is a strong offense. He's invaded Thrace and Macedon and now he's on his way to take Athens. We meet today to form a plan of action.

(*viii*) *Draft a Discussion Schedule.* Finally, draft a brief schedule for the discussion. Here is a sample discussion schedule.

- 1:00 PM. Pray, collect homework, tell everyone to put away books, Opening Script.
- 1:07 PM. Personal Stake Questions, Background Questions, Primary Question. Keep an eye on time and help them. Try to get to answering Primary Question by around 1:30.
- 1:35–1:40 PM. Success, hopefully. Give key points on Battle of Marathon. Try to tell it as a story. Don't have them take notes. That will kill the magic. We can do the notes quickly tomorrow.
- 1:40–1:50 PM. Celebrate and post-game the discussion and highlights. Time for questions.
- 1:50–1:55 PM. Assign homework reading on Battle of Marathon and to draw a picture of some aspect of the battle. Review tomorrow.

(2) REMOTE PREPARATION

(*i*) *Assign Any Necessary Reading or Research.* Assign any reading or research necessary to be able to participate in the discussion. Do not assign any reading or research that would contain "spoilers."

(*i*) *Plant Information.* If possible, "plant" information, like authors of detective fiction plant clues.

For example, here are tasks I would schedule earlier in the course so that students would have the information they need to participate in the Marathon discussion.

- In the Assyrian unit, take time to discuss differences between ancient and modern warfare. Observe and discuss what little recourse smaller nations had against invaders.
- In the Persian unit, stress Persia's military strength. Discuss Cyrus and Persia from other points of view, like Israel and in comparison with empires like Babylon or Assyria.
- Start Ancient Greece unit with geography and map-drawing. When we talk about the Trojan War and the *Iliad*, get into themes of defense, courage, love of country.

(iii) Seek Real-Life Relevant Student Experiences. In weeks or months leading up to the discussion, connect with students in conversation to see how much they know about the topic or if they have relevant or analogous experiences. For example, in preparing for the Battle of Marathon discussion, I might talk with students during lunch to see how much they know about outflanking and maneuvering. I might watch a school game to get examples of outflanking during sports and note how many of my students were present at the game.

C. *Process*

Start with your opening script. Then begin asking questions, starting with Personal Stake Questions and working through Background Questions until you arrive at and ask your Primary Question.

Volume I: *Paideia to Monastic Education*

Let the discussion be spontaneous and lively. Expect the discussion to jump back and forth across the questions. Make sure everyone has a chance to express what he knows as well as his views, questions, or concerns. It is better if students do not have to raise their hands, but you might employ the use of hand-raising if students are starting to interrupt each other. If the discussion is dragging, play devil's advocate or give the floor to a student who has adopted the devil's advocate role. Help the students as needed but try to be subtle about giving hints. Keep an eye out for frustration. Frustrated students can start to feel like this is a guessing game. They need to feel like the question has become their own and that they can successfully solve it. Offer lots of praise along the way.

Sometimes students get close to the correct answer; sometimes they succeed. It is a great moment. Reiterate and expand on the details of the day's topic with a short didactic summary. For example, tell the students how the Battle of Marathon really did play out, perhaps with a diagram and few notes on the board. Or save diagrams and notes for review the following day.

Finally, acknowledge and celebrate the success with the students. Discuss the discussion, the parts where they got confused or stuck and the moment when things "clicked" for them. Discuss where they disagreed with each other, when they changed their minds, and how they helped each other. Praise the students individually and as a group for the highlights of the discussion.

D. *Other Ideas for Socratic Discussion*

THEOLOGY

Choose a moral issue for which the Catholic Church has a specific teaching, then lead students through questions to use what they know about the Catholic Church's moral theology to discern what the Catholic Church teaches on a particular issue.

SCIENCE AND NATURAL HISTORY

If your students love nature study and going outside, you might not need to develop any Personal Stake Questions. But sometimes they add interest.

You can develop Personal Stake Questions around imaginative scenarios. Here is a sample Personal Stake Question adapted as an opening script for an imaginative scenario.

> TEACHER: We are farmers and our entire year's income is at stake. To survive, we must decide about keeping this plant, or planting this new one, etc. We must figure out the answer to this question.

You can develop Personal Stake Questions around real scenarios. Here is a sample Personal Stake Question adapted as an opening script for a real scenario.

> *Teacher*: We are going to make maple syrup. We need to tap maple trees, preferably sugar maples. How can we discern a maple from another kind

of tree now that the leaves have fallen? And if we want to tap sugar maples only, how can we distinguish them from other maples?

CHAPTER VI

Assignments, Projects, and Activities from *Paideia* to Monastic Education

~ ~

THE FABLE

The "Fable," and the next two exercises "Narrative," and "Chria" (χρεία) are adapted from Hellenistic writing exercises described by Henri Marrou in *A History of Education in Antiquity*.[1] Each strengthens memory and attention. "Fable" and "Narrative" bear some resemblance to the Charlotte Mason narrative assessments in which students relate what they have learned orally or in writing.

In the "Fable" exercise, students listen to or read a story. Then the "Fable" directs students to write word for word as much of the story as they can remember.

THE NARRATIVE

A teacher prepares students for this exercise by explaining how to identify the following elements of a story:

(1) The agent or protagonist (Who)
(2) Action (What)

---

1. Henri Marrou, *A History of Education in Antiquity*, translated by George Lamb (New York: Mentor, 1956), 239–241.

(3) Time (When)
(4) Place (Where)
(5) Manner (How)
(6) Cause (Why)
(7) Type of literature from which the passage is taken.

Then the students listen to or read a story. The "Narrative" asks students to repeat the story in their own words, briefly, clearly, and accurately. The "Narrative" also asks students to identify the following elements within the story:

(1) The agent or protagonist (Who)
(2) Action (What)
(3) Time (When)
(4) Place (Where)
(5) Manner (How)
(6) Cause (Why)
(7) Type of literature from which the passage is taken.

A teacher can ask students to complete all elements of the "Narrative" from memory or just the part that deals with retelling the story. Completed "Narratives," especially student answers for the section on "Cause (Why)" offer a good springboard for discussion.

THE CHRIA

The "Chria" calls on memory, imagination, and attention. The teacher can prepare the students by sharing information related to the elements of the "Chria" or by requiring a small amount of research.

In this exercise, students are given a short passage. For

example, Henri Marrou suggests: "Isocrates says, 'The roots of education are bitter but the fruits thereof are sweet.'" Students consider the passage and write a reflection that includes the following elements:

(1) A short biography introducing the author.
(2) One to two sentences paraphrasing the passage in the student's own words.
(3) A brief defense of the author's opinion.
(4) A proof by "contrast" refuting the contrary opinion. For example, an opinion contrary to Isocrates' statement is: "The roots of education are bitter and the fruits not worth it." The student would argue against this contrary opinion, using personal experience or an example from literature or history, producing a "proof by contrast."
(5) An illustration of the passage by analogy.
(6) An illustration of the passage by example from anecdote or history.
(7) One or more quotations from any authorities in support.
(8) And finally, a brief conclusion.

STUDIES IN WORDS

Word studies are especially useful if students are engaged in language study, learning how to read complex written arguments, or studying scripture.

Use or teach sentence diagramming to see how a word is being used in a particular context. I first learned to use sentence diagramming with my native language and then found it incredibly helpful for understanding Latin sentences.

Have students choose an interesting new word from recent reading, look up its definition and usage, and try writing a new sentence with the word. Enrich the dictionary definition of the word with some of the following exercises. Encourage students to keep a personal index of how the word is being used in a text. Ask students to explore the word's use in other contexts, for example, *Strong's Concordance* or the *Catechism of the Catholic Church* Intratext version, which lists words with their frequency and context, linked to their source. Hold a discussion on findings and fill the board with examples to illuminate how a word is being used. Have the students vote on a favorite "word of the week."

THE "ACCESSUS AD AUCTORES"

This exercise asks students to read a work and write a short reflection that includes the following elements:

(1) A short biography introducing the author.

(2) Title of the work.

(3) Writer's intention or purpose in writing the work.

(4) Subject of the work.

(5) Identification of the field to which the work belongs.

(6) Usefulness of its contents. Usefulness points to the book's success in directing the soul to God and in achieving the writer's intention. However, you might allow a student to add something additionally relevant. For example, a student might write that the usefulness of Augustine's *Confessions* lies in convincing the reader through the story that we are restless until we rest in God, a "utility" close to

Volume I: *Paideia to Monastic Education*

Augustine's intention in writing the book. But one might also write other relevant uses, for example: "This book offers a window into the early Christian attitude to pagan learning" or "This book gives one a lot to think about regarding the right way to parent adolescents."

A variation on this exercise is the Annotated Bibliography, suitable for students who have begun a course of extensive reading. This exercise asks students to write two to five hundred words describing each work they read. This reflection contains information like the "Accessus ad Auctores." It might add key words, a few sentences about the content and structure of the book, or notes useful to the student for later in life. A monk would write an "Accessus ad Auctores" partly to track and remember extensive reading. Today, since documents are word searchable, an Annotated Bibliography can be extremely helpful for teaching, writing, and projects far in the future.

SING AND PRAY

Teach and sing a piece of chant together, such as "Regina Caeli," in unison or with a drone, or the Byzantine chant-based "St. Michael the Archangel II" arranged by Paul Jernberg and David Clayton.

Teach and lead students through a sample of Lectio Divina.

Teach how to pray part of the Liturgy of the Hours aloud and then pray it together. Try Night Prayer, which is the simplest.

HANDBOOK TO THE HEART OF CULTURE

IMITATE MEDIEVAL POETRY

Explore and discuss medieval poetic texts like *Victimae Paschali Laudes* (Easter Sequence) or *Stabat Mater* (At the Cross Her Station Keeping). Assign students to try to write one or more verses of an original liturgical poem imitating the pattern of a medieval text of their choice. For example, a student might try to write a poem imitating the rhyming pattern and two-line format of *Victimae Paschali Laudes* or a poem imitating the three-line format of *Stabat Mater*.

COPY A TEXT

Allow students to choose a text. Direct them to meditate on the passage in three stages. First, they read it aloud to themselves. Next, they reread it slowly, aloud or silently, trying to imagine and reflect on what they are reading. Finally, they copy the text out by hand and decorate or illustrate the page.

THE FLORILEGIUM

Have students choose or make and decorate a blank journal. Then ask students to compile and enter personally instructive or meaningful quotations over the course of the year. Have students share favorite pages and quotations.

ENGAGE IN AN ASPECT OF MEDIEVAL BOOKMAKING

Work with students individually or as group to engage in some aspect of medieval bookmaking. For example, research images and examples of illuminated manuscripts, bestiaries, or herbaria, and show them in class. Have students see and color an illustration of an illuminated letter or manuscript

Volume I: *Paideia to Monastic Education*

image. Have students sketch and compose written descriptions of animals seen around home or school. Put these together as a class "bestiary." Bring examples of herbs (rosemary, thyme, etc.) and have students sketch or compose descriptions of them. Put these works together to create a class "herbarium."

Teach or have students try calligraphy. Have them write a verse of scripture in calligraphy or design an original illuminated letter.

For a more challenging project, explore ink making and bookbinding and use what you learn to help students compile their creations into an "illuminated manuscript." See chapter seven of the Workbook for resources to learn more about these techniques. You may also want to involve older students or other faculty from theology, literature, history, chemistry, and biology departments to collaborate on a bookmaking project.

HOLD A "DAY IN THE LIFE OF A MONASTERY"

Incorporate one or more of the ideas listed above. For example, my "Day in the Life of a Monastery" spanned a couple days. We prayed psalms from Night Prayer, drew herbs, and practiced calligraphy. We watched part of *Into Great Silence*. *Of Gods and Men* would also have been a good choice for older students. An experience of manual labor, such as working in a garden would be a good addition.

CHAPTER VII

Further Reading and Resources

~~

On Education: From Paideia to Monastic Education

Astell, Ann W. "On the Usefulness and Use Value of Books: A Medieval and Modern Inquiry." In *Medieval Rhetoric: A Casebook*, edited by Scott D. Troyan. New York: Routledge, 2004.

Augustine. *On Christian Teaching*. Translated by R. P. H. Green. New York: Oxford University Press, 1999.

Dalton, Jane E., Maureen P. Hall, and Catherine E. Hoyser. "An Ancient Monastic Practice: Reviving It for a Modern World." In *The Whole Person: Embodying Teaching and Learning Through Lectio and Visio Divina*. Lanham, MD: Rowman & Littlefield Publishers, 2019.

Dawson, Christopher. "Religion and the Life of Civilization." In *Dynamics of World History*, edited by John J. Mulloy with an introduction by Dermot Quinn. Wilmington, DE: ISI Books, 2002.

Green, Brian Patrick. "The Catholic Church and Technological Progress: Past, Present, and Future." *Religions* 8, no. 6 (2017): 106.

Hezser, Catherine. "Private and Public Education." In *The Oxford Handbook of Jewish Daily Life in Roman Palestine*. New York: Oxford University Press, 2010.

Hezser, Catherine. *Jewish Literacy in Roman Palestine*. Tübingen: Mohr Siebeck, 2001.

Marrou, Henri. *A History of Education in Antiquity*. Translated by George Lamb. New York: Sheed and Ward, 1956.

White, Carolinne, trans. *The Rule of St. Benedict*. New York: Penguin Books, 2008.

On Sensory-Emotional Formation, Wonder, and Studiousness

Adams, Gwen. "St. Jerome Academy." In *By an Unexpected Way*. Denver, CO: Augustine Institute, 2019.

Aristotle. *Politics*. In *The Basic Works of Aristotle*, edited with an introduction by Richard McKeon. New York: Random House, 1941.

Gruber, Matthias J., Bernard D. Gelman, and Charan Ranganath. "States of Curiosity Modulate Hippocampus-Dependent Learning via the Dopaminergic Circuit." *Neuron* 84, no. 2 (2014): 486–496.

Smith, Randall B. "If Philosophy Begins in Wonder: Aquinas, Creation, and Wonder." *Communio* 41, no. 1 (2014): 92–111.

On Work and Play

Brown, Stuart. "Discovering the Importance of Play through Personal Histories and Brain Images: An Interview with Stuart Brown." *American Journal of Play* 1, no. 4 (2009): 399–412.

Brown, Stuart. *Play: How It Shapes the Brain, Opens the Imagination, and Invigorates the Soul*. New York: Avery, 2009.

Henry, Todd. *The Accidental Creative: How to Be Brilliant at a Moment's Notice*. New York: Penguin Publishing Group, 2013.

John Paul II. Homily for Holy Mass at the Shrine of the Holy Cross. Mogiła, 9 June 1979.

McKeown, Greg. *Effortless: Make It Easier to Do What Matters Most*. New York: Currency, 2021.

McKeown, Greg. *Essentialism: The Disciplined Pursuit of Less*. New York: Crown, 2020.

Newport, Cal. *Deep Work: Rules for Focused Success in a Distracted World.* New York: Grand Central Publishing, 2016.

For Nature Study and Teaching How to Draw

Audubon, John James. *Audubon's Birds of America Coloring Book.* New York: Dover Publications, 1974.

Comstock, Anna Botsford. *Handbook of Nature Study.* 24th ed. Ithaca, NY: Comstock Publishing Associates, 1939.

Edwards, Betty. *Drawing on the Artist Within: An Inspirational and Practical Guide to Increasing Your Creative Powers.* New York: Simon & Schuster, 1987.

Edwards, Betty. *The New Drawing on the Right Side of the Brain.* New York: Tarcher/Putnam, 1999.

Laws, John Muir. *The Laws Guide to Nature Drawing and Journaling.* Berkley, CA: Heyday, 2016.

Ray, H. A. *The Stars: A New Way to See Them.* New York: HarperCollins, 2016.

Sloane, Eric. *Look at the Sky and Tell the Weather.* Mineola, NY: Dover, 2004. See also other illustrated books by Sloane.

Volume I: *Paideia to Monastic Education*

Watts, May Theilgaard. *Reading the Landscape of America*. Rochester, NY: Nature Study Guild Publishers, 1999.

Watts, May Theilgaard. *Tree Finder*. Rochester, NY: Nature Study Guild Publishers, 1998. See also other books based on *Tree Finder*.

Wessels, Tom. *Reading the Forested Landscape*. Woodstock, VT: The Countryman Press, 1999.

On the Quadrivium

Augros, Michael. *Introductory Geometry and Arithmetic*. Arts of Liberty. https://www.artsofliberty.org.

Caldecott, Stratford. *Beauty for Truth's Sake: On the Re-Enchantment of Education*. Grand Rapids, MI: Brazos Press, 2009.

Ulrickson, Peter. *A Brief Quadrivium*. Washington, DC: Catholic University of America Press, 2023.

For Improving Reading Aloud Skills

Bellingham, Rebecca L. *The Artful Read-Aloud: 10 Principles to Inspire, Engage, and Transform Learning*. Portsmouth, NH: Heinemann, 2020.

Bertram, Jean DeSales. *The Oral Experience of Literature: Sense, Structure, and Sound*. San Francisco: Chandler Publishing Company, 1967.

Coger, Leslie Irene, and Melvin R. White. *Readers Theatre Handbook: A Dramatic Approach to Literature*. 3rd ed. Glenview, IL: Scott, Foresman & Company, 1982.

Eisenson, Jon. *The Improvement of Speech and Diction*. New York: MacMillan, 1958.

Gottlieb, Marvin R. *Oral Interpretation*. New York: McGraw-Hill Book Company, 1980.

Laminack, Lester L. "Read Aloud Often and Well." *Voices from the Middle* 24, no. 4 (2017): 33–35.

Mayer, Lyle Vernon. "Inflection" and "Stress and Emphasis" in chapter 6, "The Expressive Voice," *Fundamentals of Voice and Articulation*. 15th ed. Dubuque, IA: McGraw-Hill Companies, 2013.

Authors or Texts to Explore for Good Read-Aloud Books

GRADES K–6
    Aesop *Fables*
    Burnett, Frances Hodgson
    Dasent, George Webbe (*East o' the Sun and West o' the Moon*)

Volume I: *Paideia to Monastic Education*

Doyle, Arthur Conan (particularly Sherlock Holmes stories)
Graham, Kenneth (*The Wind in the Willows*)
Grimm's Fairy Tales
Jacobs, Joseph (*English Fairytales* and *Celtic Fairytales*)
Kipling, Rudyard
Lewis, C. S.
Nesbit, E.
Perrault, Charles (*Fairy Tales*)
Pyle, Howard
Stevenson, R. L. (*Treasure Island*)
White, E. B.
Wilder, Laura Ingalls

GRADES 7+
Austen, Jane
Beowulf
Dickens, Charles
El Cid
Green, Roger Lancelyn, ed. *King Arthur and His Knights of the Round Table.*
Song of Roland
Stevenson, R. L. (particularly *Kidnapped* and *Dr. Jekyll and Mr. Hyde*)
Tolkien, J. R. R.
Trollope, Anthony
Wodehouse, P. G.

HANDBOOK TO THE HEART OF CULTURE

Audiobook Readers and Voice Artists to Explore for Reading Aloud

AMERICAN
- Boss, Tyler (Amen App)
- Daniels, Jeff
- Disney, Melissa (Amen App)
- Jackson, Dianne (Amen App)
- Pratt, Sean
- Seawood, James (Amen App)

BRITISH
- Cecil, Jonathan
- Chan, Joy
- Chant, Alan and Hazel
- Cousins, S. D.
- Davidson, Frederick (also read under the name David Case)
- Dobson, Cathy
- Fox, Emilia
- Fry, Stephen
- Giordani, Andrea
- Joyce, Peter Newcombe
- Larkin, Alison
- Laurie, Hugh
- May, Nadia (also read under the names Wanda McCaddon and Donada Peters)
- Molina, Alfred
- Nicholson, Mil
- Perkins, Derek

Volume I: *Paideia to Monastic Education*

Prebble, Simon
Shaw-Parker, David
Tull, Patrick
Vance, Simon
York, Michael

Guides for Liturgy of the Hours and Lectio Divina

In the United States, DivineOffice.org offers text and audio downloads to follow along with the Liturgy of the Hours.

Ebreviary.com offers the Liturgy of the Hours in Spanish and English with an option to download a PDF file (5.5" x 8.5") to be printed as booklets.

Amen App from the Augustine Institute offers Lectio Divina resources.

Hallow App offers Lectio Divina and a seven-day cycle of Night Prayer.

For Medieval Bookmaking Activities

Explore Dover Publications illuminated manuscript coloring books: *The Illuminated Manuscript* by Theodore Menten, *Illuminated Manuscripts* by Marty Noble, *Celtic Alphabet Designs* by Cari Buziak, and images from T. H. White's *The Book of Beasts: Being a Translation from a Latin Bestiary of the Twelfth Century*.

Calligrafile. Exercises and Practice Copy Sheets. https://calligrafile.com/lettering-sheets.

Logan, Jason. *Make Ink: A Forager's Guide to Natural Inkmaking.* New York: Abrams, 2018.

Val, Tanya. Articles related to "30 Days of Natural Inks" at https://www.tanyaval.com/.

Watson, Aldren A. *Hand Bookbinding: A Manual of Instruction.* New York: Dover Publications, 2012.

Wellington, Irene. *The Irene Wellington Copy Book in Four Parts: An Omnibus Edition.* London: Pentalic Corporation, 1977.

Finally, the Fitzwilliam Museum at Cambridge Archive has a pictorial explanation of how to use a medieval herringbone stitch with cords that attach to wooden board covers. See https://colour-illuminated.fitzmuseum.cam.ac.uk/rebinding/rebinding. For a more medieval book, use the techniques of Watson's book, chapter 4, "Technical Methods" but replace the fabric tape with double-linen cords or rope of a similar diameter.

CONCLUSION TO VOLUME I

THIS VOLUME pairs with *The Heart of Culture*, from the Introduction through chapter four. It surveyed the story of western education from Greek *paideia* and Jewish education to the monastic model. The Incarnation transformed the world. Disciples of Christ synthesized their educational roots to develop a model focused on the love of learning and the desire for God. Some of the hallmarks of this education included a reverence for the word and an epistemology that trained the body and the soul, the five external senses, the four interior senses, the emotions, and the intellect. This volume reflected on the virtue of studiousness guiding the emotion of wonder in an integrated sensory-emotional formation. The volume closed with practical applications adapted from the tradition: physical activity and manual labor, singing, dance, contact with nature and nature observation, reading aloud, instructing through Socratic questioning, ideas for assignments, projects, and activities, and suggestions for further reading.

Volume II will turn to the contributions of the Medieval world and the Renaissance and Baroque era, examining the ways Christians developed their educational model. The volume will reflect on the virtue of docility. When wonder has awoken, the virtue of studiousness seeks a mentor. The virtue of docility makes that mentorship possible. The volume will close with practical applications adapted from this period of Catholic education: crafting a great lecture, leading a discussion on poetry, cultivating the memory, staging a play, ideas for assignments, projects, and activities, and suggestions for further reading.

www.ingramcontent.com/pod-product-compliance
Lightning Source LLC
Chambersburg PA
CBHW052144070526
44585CB00017B/1962